HIGH-
HANGING
FRUIT

HIGH-HANGING FRUIT

Build Something Great by Going Where No One Else Will

MARK RAMPOLLA

Portfolio / Penguin

Portfolio / Penguin
An imprint of Penguin Random House LLC
375 Hudson Street
New York, New York 10014

LIBRARY OF CONGRESS CATALOGING-IN-PUBLICATION DATA

Names: Rampolla, Mark, author.
Title: High-hanging fruit : build something great
by going where no one else will / Mark Rampolla.
Description: New York : Portfolio/Penguin, [2016]
Identifiers: LCCN 2016017393 | ISBN 9780399562129 (print) |
ISBN 9780399562143 (ebook)
Subjects: LCSH: Rampolla, Mark. | Social entrepreneurship.
Classification: LCC HD60 .R348 2016 | DDC 658.4/08—dc23
LC record available at https://lccn.loc.gov/2016017393

Printed in the United States of America
10 9 8 7 6 5 4 3 2 1

Designed by Daniel Lagin
Set in Mercury Text G1 with DIN Next Rounded LT Pro

To my parents, who showed me what it means to reach higher.

CONTENTS

HIGH-
HANGING
FRUIT

CHAPTER 1
REACH HIGHER

On an unusually warm and clear Saturday morning for December in San Salvador, we drove to the beach to meet friends for the day. The air was filled with that uniquely sweet Central American scent comprising notes of jasmine, bougainvillea, tropical humidity, crushed sugar cane, and burning trash. After several years living here it now smelled like home. Maura was asleep in the passenger seat. Six months into her second pregnancy she was struggling with an all-day version of morning sickness. Ciara, our eighteen-month-old, was conked out in her rear-facing car seat behind us. My work for International Paper's (IP) packaging business had taken me to Argentina and Venezuela that previous week, and I was tired myself and looking forward to catching a few z's in one of the hammocks strung between coconut trees at the little beach house that would be our refuge for the day.

As we descended from the mountains to the coastal plain, I could feel my ears pop and the temperature rise. We drove into the sleepy port town of La Libertad. Maura awakened out of her slumber and spotted a roadside vendor, saying, *"Agua de coco!* That's something I can drink. Can we stop?" I said sure, but reminded her that we were only ten minutes from the house. "You know Jorge will have one ready for you in five minutes and you can drink it while floating in the pool."

"Ah, that sounds perfect," Maura said. "Keep going."

I pulled up to the tall blue gate we knew well and beeped twice. Jorge, the property manager, opened the gate and ushered us in. We chatted a little and I asked him if he could get us a bunch of coconuts for the day: *"Maura está un poco enferma."* He said back to me, *"Qué lastimá. Agua de coco fresca es exactamente lo que ella necesita!"*

After we parked, we watched as Jorge picked one of the coconut trees to harvest. He tightened a rope between his feet, wrapped his arms and knees around the trunk, and expertly shinnied up twenty-five feet or so to the top. He pulled out a machete from the sheath strapped to his waist and hacked away at a branch. Down fell a bunch of five or six coconuts still attached together.

By the time I helped Maura from the car and took Ciara out of her seat, Jorge had hauled the coconuts to the *palapa* by the pool. Holding one in his hand, he used the same machete to slice the husk little by little until he breached its tender shell. I took a picture of Ciara standing, staring down, fascinated at the bunch of coconuts on the ground, while Jorge put a straw inside one and handed it to Maura. She took a long drink, thanked him, and melted into one of the lounge chairs.

Within the hour, our group of friends was sitting poolside. There was Don, the deputy director of the Peace Corps, and his wife Candy, who was an executive with Save the Children. They owned the house. Dave and Terry, who both worked at the U.S. Embassy in San Salvador, were there. Lane and Kelly and their kids, who had recently moved from El Salvador to Guatemala, were the last to arrive. Lane was country director of Catholic Relief Services (CRS) and Kelly consulted for UNICEF. I loved hanging out with this group, although their professional dedication to good works and higher callings sometimes made me wonder if I was doing enough with my life.

As we floated in the pool, we chatted about typical expatriate themes: safety, the economy, local politics, and the latest stomach illnesses. Inevitably, the conversation drifted to what we planned to do next in our lives. Expats tend to be transients, usually staying only a few years in a given job or location. Most of us had been in the country for at least two years and were all beginning to plan what came next.

Dave, we learned, was being considered for a big promotion that would take him to Colombia. Terry wanted to move to Indonesia and hoped to shift from the consular section to the economic development track. Lane and Kelly talked about their dreams to move to Ecuador or Africa and continue their work for the poor. "What's next for the Rampollas?" Terry asked.

The question was timely. We'd been living in El Salvador for almost three years, and Maura and I talked constantly about the paths we might take: what was best for our young family, our careers, and us as a couple. Maura could do her public health consulting work from anywhere, but for me, I admitted, "That's a tough one."

I told them that work at IP was going well and that I'd likely soon be running all of Latin America for my division, which made it worth staying a few more years. Then I would be ready to move on, and it looked like there might be opportunities for me in Europe or Brazil.

"So it sounds like you're on your way," Terry said.

"I guess," I said, "but . . ." I looked around at the group. "The truth is that I don't know that paper and packaging is really what I want to dedicate my life to. If I leave IP, I guess my next logical career move would be to run the Latin America operations for some big U.S. company. But I know what that job would mean: We live in Miami and I travel one hundred to two hundred days per year. And for what? So I can make a ton of money for the company, some for us, work my way up the ladder, and eventually retire and spend my days golfing? That's not what either of us want, so I'm not really sure what we're going to do."

Maura, worried that I was heading into an existential crisis, chimed in: "Mark, there's a million things you can do. And yes, many of them are more interesting and inspirational than packaging."

"Maybe it's time for me to move to the nonprofit world," I said. "Maybe I'll return to the Peace Corps and take over for Don when he retires. Or Lane, could you find me something at CRS?"

"Mark, you'd be great in nonprofit but I think you'd be frustrated. Change is incremental and slow and it can be very political," Lane said. "With your background and experience I think you can make a bigger impact in the private sector."

I thought back to my Peace Corps experience as a small business development consultant in Costa Rica. No doubt, I helped change a few lives but on a frustratingly small scale. I had always struggled with how to reconcile my belief in making a social impact with my interest in business. My dad was a nuclear physicist and my mom a counselor, artist, and teacher. Morality, spiritual purpose, social responsibility, and even war and poverty in El Salvador were regular dinner table conversations in our Italian/Irish Catholic family. My parents also practiced what they preached, taking us to swim at the all-black public pool in town, bringing an unwed teenage mother to live with us, and adopting a Bosnian refugee family from the Yugoslav wars.

In college at Marquette University, I found myself drawn to study business after meeting friends with entrepreneurial parents, intrigued by their dynamic world full of challenging opportunities to shape the future and frankly to make a lot of money. This was the era of Gordon Gekko in the movie *Wall Street*, and "greed is good" was the maxim of the day. I struggled with how to reconcile what appeared to be disparate worlds. On the one hand, I wanted to become a young master of the universe. On the other, I was pulled toward my family's value of social activism and a desire to give something to the world.

After the Peace Corps, I continued to wrestle with these issues in graduate school at Duke University while pursuing joint MBA and environmental management degrees. One class would focus on profit maximization and the importance of shareholder value. In the next, I'd learn how businesses could have a devastating impact on poor communities and sensitive environments. While there I met Maura, who was pursuing her master's in public health at neighboring UNC Chapel Hill, and we soon started dating. She came from a like-minded family and held similar values but also had a magnetic and near-uncontainable *joie de vivre*. Her enthusiasm added a whole new dimension to the equation: that of having pure fun and enjoying life.

Because Maura and I were in serious debt from grad school, we decided I would take whatever job paid well and also gave me the fastest chance to actually run a business. That turned out to be old industrial International Paper. After two years of strategy and business development in their corporate headquarters in Memphis, Tennessee, and traveling to Europe, Latin America, and Asia, I was offered an opportunity to run a business in El Salvador and we jumped at it.

Now, three years later we had "made it" by most traditional standards. We were happily married and building a family. My salary allowed us to pay down all of our debt, have a big house and a staff of three. I ran a multinational business with three hundred employees and was meeting with presidents, ambassadors, and dignitaries of various countries. I was on the fast track to the highest executive ranks of a Fortune 100 company. Maura consulted with public-health nonprofits and supported rural community projects. We dined in the finest restaurants, vacationed in exotic spots, contributed to worthy charities. I also considered myself (and believe others did, too) a good and ethical businessperson. We had it all. *Or did we?*

Sometimes, the closer you get to your goals, the more you realize they're not really your goals.

As I talked with our friends that day, I knew clearly that something was missing. I was beginning to see the limitations of achieving "success" in business—at least how success had been traditionally defined. I noticed many others who had achieved so-called success sacrifice their personal health and destroy relationships with friends and family or make decisions that negatively affected the lives of dozens or thousands of people. Most businesspeople I knew were passionately competitive, but very few I met could give me a compelling answer to why they were playing the game in the first place.

"Don't worry about it, *amor*. We'll figure it out," Maura reassured me. "Instead let's focus on the here and now. May I have another *agua de coco* with a little *limón, por favor*? The *bebecita* and I are parched. What in the world will we do without coconut water when we move back to the States someday?"

Of course, at the time, we had no idea that we were holding the literal seed of a great idea right there in our hands. I certainly had no idea I would quit my lucrative job, we would move to New York, launch Zico, and struggle for years just to survive without knowing if we had risked it all for nothing. In that moment, we couldn't have imagined that we would help to catalyze an eight-billion-dollar global industry that would revolutionize the beverage industry, contribute to the health and wellness of millions of consumers, and lead to billions of dollars of investment in developing countries and the employment of hundreds of thousands of people. We didn't know we would build a great team and engage yogis, nutritionists, celebrities, and athletes to help tell our story. And we certainly had no idea that in addition to achieving conventional success and greater financial freedom than we could have imagined, this whole process would strengthen our marriage and family, improve my health, and help us to become more spiritual and realize what was truly important in life. Yet, when I think about how it all started, my mind goes back to the memory of watching Maura, six months pregnant, drink down the water from those freshly harvested coconuts that day by the pool.

The idea was right there over our heads. We just had to reach a little higher.

My journey from Peace Corps volunteer to corporate executive to becoming an entrepreneur was fundamentally motivated and guided by the pursuit of something higher. It was about more than money, more than conventional success. We achieved those, too, but they were the low-hanging fruit. Not to say they were at all easy, but they were more obvious goals. Right there, in front of us. Fortunately, by reaching higher, we achieved so much more. Building Zico and pursuing these higher goals wasn't easy, and the path was never straight or clear. Maura and I navigated through the heart-wrenching pains of start-up mode; the all-consuming intensity of building a new brand; brutal competition; and all the physical, mental, emotional, and moral challenges that the modern business world could throw at us. Yet we survived and in fact achieved more than we ever could have dreamed, well beyond the typical entrepreneurial success story.

In that often-told story, an entrepreneur finds some brilliant way to do something ten times better, faster, or cheaper than what was on the market before. They launch a risky new business with the goal of capturing a big chunk of some huge market dominated by a corporate behemoth. They face many challenges along the way but power through with brute force and determination to capture the hearts and minds of their customers. They go on to build a hugely profitable business, take their company public, sell to a corporate buyer, or stay at the helm for a lifetime. They amass a personal fortune, buy the big house on the hill and a ranch in Montana and fill them with art and all the toys. They vacation on yachts in the French Riviera or in rural eco-lodges in Cambodia or just "hang" with their celebrity friends in the Swiss Alps. They're interviewed by *Fast Company, Wired*, and *Fortune*, and get invited to speak at TED, Aspen, Davos, or Summit Series to share their secrets to success. To "give back," they start a foundation, fund a new building for their college, support worthy causes, and commit to giving away 50 percent of their wealth before they die. What more could a modern entrepreneur want?

We often celebrate entrepreneurs who are willing to lay it all on the line for success. Yet all too often you can "win" by the conventional measures while betraying your personal values and some deep human needs like your desire to experience joy, creativity, fun, spirituality, beauty, and love on a daily basis. It's possible to cruise off into the sunset after damaging the health of your consumers, profiting unfairly from the work of employees or suppliers, burning through precious resources, leaving a wake of environmental devastation, and leading a life utterly lacking in awareness and contemplation and filled instead with an obsessive pursuit of "just a little more."

Maura and I count ourselves among a generation of entrepreneurs and business leaders who are reaching for something higher. We reject the old adage, "Nothing personal. It's just business." In fact, we put our hearts and souls into making our businesses fundamentally and deeply personal. Success requires that our ventures reflect our individual values, personal priorities, and passions. Entrepreneurs who are guided by this sort of reliable internal compass are those who produce the products and services that make the world a better place while simultaneously minimizing their negative impact. They build businesses that have an uplifting, positive impact on everyone—including the founder(s), employees, families, suppliers, business partners, and investors—not just in some distant future but throughout the journey.

Not only are we *not* willing to sacrifice our marriages, families, friendships, passions, health, and values for business success, we expect our ventures to enhance our families, strengthen our relationships, and align with our dreams, passions, and life ambitions. We are convinced our professional life must nourish us on a level far deeper than simply putting food on the table and money in the bank. We view our ventures as an opportunity to learn about ourselves: our strengths, weaknesses, values, and priorities. The idea of success for us is not a distant, hoped-for payout but something we work to experience continuously. In fact, if the daily journey of creating your business is a meaningful, challenging, and personal quest, it becomes an endeavor where you literally cannot lose. Regardless of the business's eventual success or failure by conventional measures, the adventure will have been worth it, and the world will be a better place because you set and worked toward your intention. This is what I mean by reaching higher.

Do those seem like high-minded goals that might make starting or succeeding in business even more difficult than it already is? I argue—and here is the key counterintuitive argument of this book—that your chances of "winning" by conventional measures are *far more likely* if you reach higher from day one. Passion is a magnet for the best and brightest talent. Great employees want to work for bosses who are driven by high personal standards and have the enthusiasm of being on a personal mission. Many investors are looking for these entrepreneurs as well, seeking to make an impact with their capital while they generate reasonable returns. Most importantly, today's informed and engaged consumer is tired of being pandered and talked down to. They are scouring the marketplace for products and services that offer something meaningful. All these factors make this new breed of entrepreneurs dangerous to the established corporate order. They are poised to disrupt whole industries—from energy, transportation, financial services, and health care to apparel, technology, media, and food and beverage.

The old guard will fight back and they won't always fight fair. They'll deploy advertising designed to manipulate consumers, promote unfair regulations, attempt to control routes to market, and employ armies of lawyers to defend their turf. But all these tactics will only delay the inevitable. Major corporations will either lose fighting these insurgent players or be forced to assimilate their values and mission.

High-hanging fruit is not just about an incremental change to the old way of doing business. While social responsibility was an important step for major corporations to adopt, it is often used to justify, ameliorate, or offset the negative consequences of regular business practices, with profit remaining the only true bottom line. Social entrepreneurship generally attempts to use business to achieve social objectives, and expands the concept of the bottom line to include people and the planet. But the entrepreneurs I'm talking about set out as a given that their businesses must contribute to larger social goals and minimize environmental impact, and also add a new dimension to the triple bottom line: that of finding deeper meaning through business by pursuing one's highest and best use and helping others do the same.

This revolution is poised to disrupt the world by combining the power of entrepreneurship with deep personal values, purpose, and mission. Since we launched Zico in 2004 we have witnessed hundreds and know there are thousands of other entrepreneurs following a similar path. No longer do the winners have to be Harvard dropouts or serial entrepreneurs who can trace their business genius back to their days of franchising lemonade stands around the neighborhood. They might begin as teachers, backwoods craftsmen, social activists, environmentalists, small farmers, anthropologists, Jesuit priests, or cancer-surviving moms. I believe that most of our shared social problems, from the economic boom and bust cycles to income and development inequalities to environmental degradation, can best be addressed through this new style of entrepreneurship. This is capitalism 2.0, and we're only at the beginning of this movement.

High-Hanging Fruit is not a how-to book or a step-by-step instructional manual. It is not a rigorous scientific study across multiple test cases. This story is my personal reflection on the journey of attempting to build a business with these higher goals in mind. It's about one person's, one couple's, one team's attempt to reach higher. I will offer lessons, thoughts, and insights I've gained in attempting to disrupt an industry ruled by a few dominant players. I'll share our intentions and triumphs, as well as my doubts, fears, and mistakes along the way as we tried to change the way business is done.

People talk a lot about the importance of being true to your values and seeking something beyond material rewards in other areas like art, music, writing, science, teaching, and drama. It is time to apply this maxim to business: to see business as an equally noble pursuit measured by more than just a single dimension. That's what this movement is about. If you choose to join us, your life, the lives of those around you, and the legacy of capitalism will never be the same, and the next generation will thank you for it. Good luck and reach higher.

CHAPTER 2
HOW GREAT IDEAS ARE SOMETIMES RIGHT OVERHEAD

"How flexographic printing is changing the world" was the name of the seminar I was sitting in on at a conference on printing and packaging in Miami, Florida, the winter of 2003. I was still a young mid-level executive with International Paper and so bored by the presenter I wondered what I was doing with my life.

That night before I flew back home to El Salvador the following morning, I had dinner in South Beach with David Andrade, who worked for me as controller for one of the five IP beverage-packaging plants I ran at the time. We sat at one of the swanky restaurants on Collins Avenue, enjoying the ocean breeze.

David and I ordered martinis and talked in Spanish about the conference and work in general. On the second round, we talked about our families and friends. On the third, we opened up and began to really talk about life, our hopes and dreams. At the time, I wouldn't usually have conversations with employees that were so personal and revealing, but David had become a good friend and would soon move on to a job in the U.S., so I felt more comfortable being candid. No doubt the three martinis helped loosen my tongue a bit.

"So, Mark, everyone knows you're not gonna stay in El Salvador forever," David said to me. "You'll get promoted or recruited by some other big company, but what I want to know is this—have you ever thought about leaving and starting your own business?"

The truth was that I had thought a good deal about joining a start-up, probably as the general manager or CEO who took over from an entrepreneur with a brilliant idea. Over the last ten years, I had become confident in my business skills. I was the guy who could build and lead teams, develop strategies, execute plans, reach goals, get things done. I could see myself taking a company from $1 million to $10 million, or $10 million to $100 million, or maybe even $100 million to $1 billion. But in those dreams, I never cast myself as the founder, the person who had come up with the new idea.

"I'm not really the idea guy," I said, looking out toward the night sky. "I've got friends who are always coming up with new products or services. That's not me. But I would love to find someone with an idea I can believe in and passionately get behind. Assuming we can find the money we need, I think I could figure out the strategy and scale it."

When I looked back at David, he had a funny, expressionless face as if I had just said something idiotic. "Mark," he said, gesturing around at the lively South Beach social scene, "the only difference between you and an entrepreneur is an idea, and you are as capable as anyone of coming up with one."

Despite the effects of three martinis, David's simple statement hit me like a lightning bolt. Why had I been telling myself that I wasn't creative or smart enough to come up with an idea?

And when exactly had I convinced myself that creativity and follow-through were mutually exclusive? As a kid and even a teen, I had thought of myself as creative. In fact, one of my declared career goals, when asked, was to be an artist. My family had often referred to me as "project boy" for all the crazy schemes I pursued. But somewhere along the way I had persuaded myself that I was a left-brained thinker: a doer, not a dreamer. But was that just a stereotype I had imposed on myself?

With David's simple observation, I had been given permission to ignore the story I had been telling myself for decades and began a new one of possibility. A switch flipped in my brain, and I couldn't turn it off even if I wanted to. I suddenly couldn't stop thinking of new business ideas.

IDEAS ARE A DIME A DOZEN

With David's challenge echoing in my mind, I did what I always do: I dove in deep. On the plane ride back home to El Salvador, I began to make a list of ideas. I remembered a mantra I had often heard in brainstorming meetings: "There are no bad ideas." By the end of the plane ride, I had already jotted down two dozen. I got three more walking by the airport stores and kiosks. Over the following weeks the list grew longer each day. The world suddenly seemed full of opportunities to start businesses. Why, I wondered, had I not done this before? David was right; not only could I come up with a great idea, I was an idea machine.

Maura was happy that I was feeling so energized and excited. She knew me, in some ways better than I knew myself, and saw that the corporate career path I was on was becoming less and less fulfilling.

Of course, I knew that whatever business I pursued, I needed and wanted full buy-in from Maura. So one evening, a couple of weeks into my manic brainstorming, I brought out my notebook after the girls went to sleep.

Sitting on our patio overlooking the city lights, I flipped through my pages of notes and started with one I knew was a winner. "I want to consolidate the dairy industry across Central America." I let the sheer brilliance of that sit in the air for a minute, and then went on to explain that in the seven countries of Central America, with a combined population of about thirty million and an economy the size of Ohio, there were twenty-five independent dairies, none of which were large enough to be efficient. The opening of free trade with the U.S. had undercut small-scale corn growers in Mexico. The same could happen with dairy farmers in Central America, I told her. I already knew most of the players, as the business I ran for International Paper supplied the paper cartons for the milk. The small-scale milk producers were all at risk unless they consolidated and ran more efficiently. "Dean Foods revolutionized the dairy industry in the U.S.," I finished, "and we could do the same in Central America."

Maura thought for a moment, nodding her head.

"Dairy," she said, looking at me, both puzzled and bemused, "you've hidden your passion for the dairy industry from me all these years. Let me ask you this: besides the opportunity to make money, why do we want to be in that business? So we can go to more boring Dairy Federation trade shows in Chicago? Isn't that sort of the industry you're trying to get out of? How is this important for you and me and the girls and the rest of the world?"

"Well," I said, suddenly feeling like I was being attacked, "the girls drink milk." Maura cocked her head at me, indicating the lameness of the answer. Trying to get my momentum back, I doubled down and tried to convince her that there was a fortune to be made in dairy.

"Okay, I believe you," she said, interrupting my lecture. "You can make a lot of money from consolidating dairies. Is that your main point?"

Clearly, this idea didn't impress her. I flipped through the pages looking for a better one.

"Okay. What about trucking?" This one I was pretty sure would wow her because I had become something of an expert on regional trade. I was a board member for the American Chamber of Commerce of El Salvador and we were active in the negotiations of the Central American Free Trade Agreement between Central America and the U.S. One of the expected problem areas was trucking. I reminded Maura that there had been a boom in the trucking business when the U.S., Mexico, and Canada signed the North American Free Trade Agreement (NAFTA) and that the same was expected in Central America when this new agreement was signed. The trucking infrastructure that existed across the region was poor, limited, and inefficient. I knew this well as the business I ran shipped packaging across the region, and it took days and was triple the cost to ship from San Salvador to San José, Costa Rica, than from New York to Pittsburgh, roughly the same distance.

"So I'll raise some money," I said to Maura, "buy a couple of the best trucking companies, and then figure out how to make them world-class with new technology, best practices, good benefits for drivers, better safety."

"Hmm," she said. "Trucking?" All the questions she had asked before hung in the air. "Tell me, what is it about trucking that excites and inspires you?"

"Um," I stalled, knowing that I would likely regret anything that came out of my mouth.

"Trucking just doesn't do it for me," she said, reaching out her hand for the list as I surrendered it. She read aloud idea after idea: shopping malls in Honduras, clothing manufacturing in Colombia, ecotourism in Costa Rica, exporting chocolate from Belize. When she got to trucking again she was laughing so uncontrollably she couldn't keep reading.

"All right now, I admit some of these aren't that great, but don't you know the first principle of brainstorming is there are no bad ideas?" I said, taking the notepad back but laughing with her at the same time.

"Well." She paused, taking a breath and regaining control of herself. "What we're doing here is the step *after* brainstorming when we cull the herd. I don't want to squash your excitement for becoming an entrepreneur and I have no doubt if you decided to launch one of these businesses you could succeed. But if we're going to mortgage our lives to launch a business, it needs to be something we can both be passionate about. What about all the stuff we've talked about, Mark? Having fun, traveling to great places, making a positive impact on the world? Where does that fit into any of these ideas?"

I looked back at my list, scanning it for ideas by which I could redeem myself. As moneymaking business ventures, I could make the case for all of them, but I could now see that they were hollow—and might lead me and us to the same exact unfulfilled spot I was in now. Making money was important to both Maura and me. We had our girls to support, after all. And we both wanted to become financially independent enough to be comfortable in life. But the truth was that we could work toward those monetary goals without leaving the career path I was on and taking on the risks and difficulties of starting something. To start a new business required that the venture profit us, and the world, in other ways as well. Maura was reminding me that the right idea had to have a motivation deeper and higher than just typical business success and making money.

A HIGHER FORM OF IDEATION

As I thought about Maura's questions, I realized I was starting from the wrong place. I had fixated on the business opportunities I perceived needed to be filled instead of leading with more fundamental and meaningful personal questions: What problem in the world do we want to address? What impact do we want to make? What meaningful good or service do I want to contribute? What do I have to uniquely offer to the world?

For some people, the question of what they have to offer the world is relatively straightforward. We all love the stories of prodigies who show amazing aptitude at a young age—the adolescent violin virtuoso or the ten-year-old physicist—people who seem to be born great at something. At the other end of the spectrum are those who don't really care about what they produce, so long as it has a market and is profitable, much like a celebrity CEO who might be a keen manager, wiz with numbers, and gladiator at the negotiation table, motivated to win big for his or her team, whatever team that is. Despite being an icon of success, his or her story answers all the important questions about achieving remarkable success except the most important one: why?

Most of us, myself included, fall somewhere in between. We weren't born with some preternatural talent to offer the world, and yet we want careers that are more than simply maximizing income and our social status. Increasingly, we expect our professional endeavors to line up with our values, interests, personal histories, and beliefs. We want to have a clear and deeply satisfying answer to the question, "Why did you spend all that time and effort producing that product or service or starting that company?"

Of course, keeping this question in mind from the beginning will help you avoid getting off track. But that requires you to examine your personal history and inner desires to see what truly interests you. What are your talents, abilities, and passions? What excites you? What local or world problems would you like to try to solve? While you may not find *the* perfect idea or lifelong passion, with some hard work you can greatly narrow the field and select an idea that closely aligns with who you are, when you are at your best, and who you want to become.

After that evening with Maura, I put my brainstorming notepad aside and over the following weeks Maura and I took long hikes together in some of our favorite spots around San Salvador. Instead of going straight for the big idea, we discussed our personal lives, histories, and dreams. We retold stories to each other of our families, people who influenced us and whom we admired. We examined supposedly "successful" people whose lives we never wanted to emulate. We reflected on when we were happiest, when we had the most fun, our proudest moments, and the dreams we had for ourselves and our girls. We weighed the pros and cons of continuing our nomadic expat lifestyle and discussed various countries, states, and cities where we might want to put down roots.

As we talked, several guiding principles and key shared interests bubbled up right away. We had both grown up in religious households that emphasized our shared responsibility to others, especially the poor and underserved. We realized that this upbringing had shaped us substantially. Maura had dedicated herself to causes and organizations beginning in college to help people who didn't have the same advantages she had. She said it kept her grounded whether tutoring inmates at Cook County Jail, comforting AIDS hospice patients in Chicago, or being a camp counselor for intellectually challenged kids. She worked and volunteered for nonprofits and then pursued a master's degree in public health. After graduate school, she worked in various capacities championing women's and children's health and education. For me, my parents helped me develop my moral compass, which influenced my decision to attend a Jesuit college and subsequently join the Peace Corps. I lived in rural Costa Rica for two years, where I worked with small business owners, mostly single mothers, to help them grow their businesses through access to micro loans. When I returned home, I couldn't see myself just getting an MBA so I also pursued an environmental management degree. While in El Salvador we built houses with Habitat for Humanity, supported schools in poor communities, and planted trees in urban areas. Whatever business we started, we determined we didn't want to intentionally harm others or the environment and ideally wanted to make a positive impact on people's lives and health.

We also talked about how we wanted to stay healthy both for our own longevity and happiness as well as to be good role models for our girls. We were active and into biking, hiking, skiing, swimming, and yoga. We were part of a generation that was becoming ever more keenly aware of the interplay between mental, physical, and spiritual health.

And while we were passionate about our own health, we also shared a concern about health trends at large. From our expat perspective, we could easily observe how the relative wealth most Americans enjoyed guaranteed neither health nor happiness. In fact, in many ways you could make the case that America's wealth was part of the problem. Like a junkie that had won the lottery, a large portion of the population appeared to be intent on literally killing itself with unhealthy food, lifestyle choices, and stress. Those choices, it was also clear, were being shaped by a food industry that promoted and glamorized the unhealthiest foods and beverages imaginable. Obesity rates were skyrocketing in America, growing from one quarter of the population in 1990 to nearly a third just over a decade later. That drastic rise was costing people their health, but it was costing the rest of us a great deal, too. The annual medical costs and impact on economic productivity of preventable conditions were running into the hundreds of billions of dollars.

Worse yet, these unhealthy lifestyle choices started gaining momentum in the rest of the world as the U.S. exported them through media, and big food. Globalizing the American style of overconsumption and poor health habits could lead the world into deep trouble, which deeply troubled us.

Maura and I also talked about our passion for travel and how we never wanted to lose our deep love for and connection with Latin America. We had learned from the remarkable generosity and community spirit of hundreds of people we had met across Central America. Despite having suffered civil wars, natural disasters, and years of unrest, these communities managed to stay focused on what was best about us as humans—maintaining strong social bonds and creating remarkable music, literature, visual art, and food. Our family's diet had changed and been significantly enriched since moving south of the border. The local markets were filled with fresh, seasonal vegetables and fish. We became connoisseurs of fruits that we had never seen in the U.S. and knew only by their Spanish names. Our girls were reared on fresh-pressed juices and blended vegetables. Our immersion in Latin American culture enriched our lives immeasurably, and we loved sharing what we had learned with families and friends who visited us.

After a few weeks of dreaming and reflecting together, I was ready to revisit business ideation from quite a different starting point. Instead of brainstorming potential gaps in different industries, I made a list of screens, worded as questions, by which I could filter out business ideas that would not have a chance of passing what I started to call the "Maura test."

First were personal screens, questions that rose out of the conversations we had had on our walks—our individual values, histories, and interests. Was a business idea consistent with our values and lifestyle, and did it contribute to our personal goals and dreams? Would it directly and positively affect lives beyond ours? Would the world be better off if we succeeded? Would we think the project was worth it even if we failed? Would it have a positive (or at least neutral) environmental impact? Would it keep us tied to Latin America? Could I commit to this for the long term? At thirty-four years old at the time, I realized I had never held one job or stayed in one place for more than about two years. From my research I knew that launching a business successfully was a minimum five-year process and that I'd better be prepared to commit for a decade. This project would very likely define my career and in meaningful ways become my identity, so I'd better pick carefully. What would the girls think about this business when they're ten? Sixteen? Twenty-five? Forty? If we were successful (or not), would the girls be proud that we had started it? Would they be interested in working there someday? These screens wouldn't apply to everyone but they were critical to us, informed by what we had reflected on and determined as most important to us. We were now taking ideation way beyond dairy and trucking.

The second set of screens were classic MBA-style ways to evaluate the potential and viability of a business. Is it audacious? Is it a big idea that captures our hearts and those of others? Could we attract top talent and rally employees, investors, and customers around it? Is it something we were excited to talk about? If I was going to dedicate a good part of my life to something, why not do something that's a BHAG (Big, Hairy, Audacious Goal), as Jim Collins says. Does it have high gross and profit margins? I had run paper and packaging businesses with low margins, and I can tell you it's tough! I wanted to be in a business that had higher margins to work with, which would allow us to pay people well and generate critical cash flow to fuel growth. Would it have strong growth potential? I knew we would start small, but why should it stay that way? It should be something that could grow continuously for years to come and potentially become a billion-dollar business. Could we differentiate? Is it new to the world or at least different from what's out there today? I realized that the really exciting businesses were innovative, differentiated, disruptive.

With these two sets of screens, we now had a framework to evaluate the many ideas I was generating, which only stimulated more. I compiled all of my ideas in a spreadsheet, and then evaluated them individually against the screens, which gave us context and common ground to discuss them. These screens also helped me avoid suggesting ideas that would never pass the Maura test. Coconut water was on the list from the beginning, but only by developing and using these screens did it eventually rise to the top. How did it get there and what made it bubble up to the top?

WHY COCONUT WATER?

In his autobiography, Mark Twain wrote, "There is no such thing as a new idea. It is impossible. We simply take a lot of old ideas and put them into a sort of mental kaleidoscope. We give them a turn and they make new and curious combinations." What we often think of as new ideas are actually combinations of pre-existing observations or a new connection between ideas that already exist. But at the same time, looking through the shifting colors and mirrored images of a kaleidoscope can make the world become amazing and new.

The idea of marketing coconut water, I'll be the first to admit, was not a new one. As Maura and I discovered through our travels, in certain latitudes the product couldn't be more ubiquitous. In El Salvador, we encountered it literally every day. And although it could already be found in steel cans in the ethnic aisles of some American supermarkets, in 2003 few seemed to see the billion-dollar market potential of importing the product as a mainstream drink for health-thirsty Americans.

That this opportunity escaped the notice of so many is worth pondering for a moment. How many millions of business leaders, executives, entrepreneurs, development workers, and travelers have vacationed in Latin America, the Caribbean, or the South Pacific and sipped out of a freshly cut coconut? How many more lived near the equator, where their jobs were to bring regional products to the North American market? A billion-dollar idea was resting in the palm of their hands or just overhead. Why didn't they see it?

For a tourist, the coconut as a food, drink, and object is an interesting novelty happily experienced but easily forgotten. But for tropical cultures around the world, the many uses of the coconut run much deeper: so deep in fact that they are taken for granted.

I first experienced some of that cultural connection to coconut water during my Peace Corps years in Costa Rica beginning in 1991. Relying on it as a safe and clean source of hydration was actually written into the Peace Corps manual. In our training classes we learned that coconut water can often be the best source of clean water in remote locations and that it could be used as an oral rehydration solution when someone came down with the inevitable stomach illness.

In Costa Rica you'd always see the chest-high stacks of coconuts, with a little stand behind, along the sides of the beach roads. Often these coconuts were already partially dehusked and the vendor would just cut off a small flap of the soft shell at the top and pop in a straw. You could take the whole coconut, drink the water, and then scrape out and eat the tender white meat. Sometimes the coconuts were kept in a little ice chest and the vendor would pour the water into a plastic bag with the meat floating inside. Local kids made pocket money shinnying up trees to pick coconuts for tourists on the beach.

The taste of coconut water had to grow on me, as it does for many, but soon I came to love the smooth and refreshing flavor. I remember taking a coconut on a hike up a volcano, machete in hand to protect against snakes and for splitting coconuts. I was also familiar with, let's say, less-health-conscious uses. Coconut water was a great mixer with local rum. Coincidentally, around this time, I also learned there was no better cure for a hangover.

During my backpacking through Central America post–Peace Corps I realized coconut water was not just a Costa Rican phenomenon but also a region-wide staple. Traveling through many parts of Central America pushes even the hardiest traveler's intestinal resistance, and I was grateful for a fresh coconut as something I could keep down. While working in Mexico on a summer internship during graduate school, I saw it on beaches and roadside stands. I passed out once at work from dehydration while there due to a stomach illness and awoke to my co-workers holding a coconut in front of me ready to drink.

Since most of my customers at IP were juice or dairy companies, I usually had beverages on my mind. In the hopes of finding ideas to help them grow (so we could sell more packaging), my team and I would discuss ideas for potential innovation outside of the typical milk and orange juice most of our customers sold. Rarely did they take our advice (IP is a great company but not exactly known as a beverage innovation powerhouse) but the possibility of new beverages, whether made from hibiscus flower, mango, or guava juice, or coconut water, all made it on my new list.

As I began to dig into every idea on our list, my knowledge of coconut water grew. I learned that coconuts grow in eighty-five countries across the tropical world. Humans' relationship with the drupe (as the coconut is technically categorized) likely goes as far as human existence itself. The uses are many: The meat is used in cooking, baking, and candies across the world, and the oil is also prized for both cooking and a variety of skincare remedies. The husk is used to make carpets, sandals, and as ground cover or mattress stuffing. The fronds serve as roofing material or are woven into baskets. The trunks are used for their flexible, dense wood. I learned that the magical water inside was so pure and in balance with the human body that there were well-documented accounts of it being used in place of plasma by doctors during World War II as drip IVs in the South Pacific and also in subterranean hospitals by the Vietcong during the Vietnam War.

Despite the fact that there were already millions of hectares of coconuts planted (or growing wild) across the world and a multimillion-dollar market from their oil, meat, and fiber, interestingly, the water was usually discarded as a by-product. Across the world, farmers were letting coconuts rot on the ground if prices weren't high enough, while in the oil and coconut meat facilities they would literally let the water flow down the drains as waste. What did make its way to market as coconut water (or sometimes called juice) was mostly sold straight from the coconut on a small scale. The small volume canned and shipped to the U.S. or Europe was often of poor quality, with added sugar and preservatives and cooked in a crude and damaging processing system. The sales volume exported prior to 2004 was at most in the low tens of millions of dollars in the U.S. per year, so not a big market.

I began to assess whether coconut water could become a viable business. From keeping track of trends back in the U.S., I knew a multitude of new healthy beverages, including Vitaminwater, were getting lots of press and trying to go up against Gatorade or carbonated soft drinks. So, on a trip to New York, I tried Vitaminwater. The packaging and branding were unique, and the brand was definitely playing to an audience that wanted something healthier. But reading the label I realized that at its core, this drink was little more than sugar water, and though it had natural ingredients, it was still made by some guys in a lab. I expected (incorrectly for about ten years) that sophisticated consumers would also realize the health claims were questionable and reject the drink. I thought coconut water was better and realized that if we made it hip, cool, and tasty, the market opportunity might be enormous: we could market a wholly natural version of Gatorade.

Given all our connections to the product, coconut water ended up on the short list of ideas. The more I looked at it, the more appealing it became. But would it pass the Maura test?

Coconut water and the business we would build around it fit us personally: It was a natural product, from the tropics, and could be positioned around health, wellness, and sports. It would positively affect consumers' lives by providing a healthier alternative to so many of the high-calorie, high-sugar, artificial beverages. If done correctly, we could also build a brand that would contribute to the growing cultural concern with health and active living.

Coconut water could also have a massive positive economic impact across the developing world; perhaps more and better than coffee someday given that the water wasn't the easiest product to process or transport. With its low acidity level and high enzyme content, it spoils quickly after being exposed to the air. It would require higher-paying handling, processing, and packaging jobs locally, whereas most of the value added to coffee is in the roasting process done in the U.S. or Europe. The scale of existing coconut production was already massive—on the scale of oranges—so theoretically no additional land was needed to build a multibillion-dollar industry, so the environmental impact could be negligible. There might even be positive benefits of taking that water out of the waste stream and rivers. I could clearly imagine our girls thinking it was pretty cool that their parents launched a brand that catalyzed a whole coconut water industry and helped the developing world where it originated (and they were born).

Looked at in one way, going up against Gatorade, which was already a massive global brand, was certainly audacious. Owned by

PepsiCo, Gatorade had been focus-grouped and test-marketed extensively over the years. But looked at another way, we were way ahead. We had a product that had been tested by humans around the globe for tens of thousands of years. We didn't have to patent a new formula, make sure it was healthy, or even do the basic manufacturing. It was already being manufactured by nature just about everywhere you looked if you were anywhere near a tropical coast.

We could likely source high-quality, minimally processed coconut water and build our brand as a premium one so we had the right sort of margin structure. If we could capture a fraction of Gatorade's market or even a portion of the size of soy milk or other categories, a coconut water brand could easily be a business over $100 million in sales in a reasonable number of years. Differentiating from Gatorade and the proliferation of other sports drinks would be relatively easy. We had a claim on a manifestly healthy and natural drink that they simply couldn't match. The fact that this idea was grounded in our own personal experience and values would also give us a critical advantage, we believed.

As we got more excited about the idea, we began to get feedback from friends and family. On a visit back to the U.S. around this time, I remember a conversation I had with my father-in-law when he asked me what my hopes for the new business were. Without a beat, I told him my dream. "In twenty years I want to see kids everywhere drinking coconut water, regardless of the brand, instead of high-sugar, artificial junk and in general leading healthier, more active lives," I said, rapid fire. "I want tens of thousands of people in developing countries to benefit from well-paying jobs in a healthy, sustainable, and growing coconut industry. I want our brand to live forever and stand for healthy, natural, active living, and I want everyone involved with the business to have the opportunity to learn, earn, contribute, and grow."

Silence followed. "Wow, that's ambitious," he said finally. "I thought you were just going to tell me you wanted to make a pile of dough."

I had to laugh. "To be honest," I said, "I want that, too. I believe if we do all the things I just listed, we're more likely to make that pile of dough. We'll also have something to really celebrate if we achieve it all!"

Now that I'm no longer running Zico and have invested behind dozens of entrepreneurs after listening to countless pitches, I understand how important it is to base one's business in personal passions, mission, history, and beliefs. My first questions to many entrepreneurs, after they've gone through their carefully prepared Power-Points, often catches them off guard. Why, I ask them, create this particular business above all others? Why do you want to spend your life doing this? How will it make your life better? How will it make the world better? Very few expect these questions, much like I hadn't when Maura first posed them to me, but I can honestly tell you that the entrepreneurs who have meaningful answers to these questions are the ones I get the most excited about. They've looked beyond profits and deeply within themselves, which I have found improves the probability of their success.

So now that coconut water looked like a viable idea to me, I knew I had to get buy-in from others. I figured I would test-drive my pitch with a friendly (though not weak) audience. Maura and I met my sister, Mary Beth, in the Bay Islands of Honduras for a weekend getaway. At some point sitting on the beach watching the sunset, I gave them each a freshly picked coconut, and pitched them the idea that coconut water was our breakout idea. We would develop and launch a coconut water brand and attempt to create a whole new category in the U.S. first, and then the rest of the world.

We discussed the potential impact and scale, how well it aligned with what we wanted to accomplish in life. At some point we started to get down to brass tacks. Maura asked, "So exactly where and how are we going to produce it and ensure high and consistent quality?" I admitted that I didn't have a good answer to that yet. Mary Beth asked how we would go to market, what I knew about distribution and retailers, and how it would actually get on store shelves. More good questions. Maura asked what kind of marketing we would need to do and how much money we'd need to raise and where that would come from. I started taking notes.

The more I thought about it, the more I realized that I knew near nothing about the beverage industry. Yes, I was a supplier of beverage cartons and knew about packaging and a little about processing, but launching an actual beverage would be a whole new world. I had studied some of this for my MBA but I had no practical experience with product development, branding, consumer marketing, distribution, or retail sales—in short, everything it takes to start and run a consumer product business. But I knew how to learn and decided it was time for a crash course in the beverage industry.

CHAPTER 3
LEARN FROM THOSE WHO CLIMBED BEFORE

So let's say you've done the hard work of coming up with a big idea, one that both fits with your values and principles and can make the world a better place. You're excited and energized and ready to dive in, but as you begin to think more about it and talk it over with friends or family, you hit your first major roadblock: a full realization of just how many competitors you'll face. No matter what industry you're in, I can guarantee that the marketplace is crowded and the competition fierce. Once you realize this, your confidence may waver and you may even think about giving up before you've really begun.

I fought through this roadblock not long after I began to get excited about coconut water. I hadn't yet quit my day job when a business trip brought me to New York. I skipped out of a couple of meetings one afternoon to wander into Fairway Market on the Upper West Side. Walking into a massive American supermarket, particularly if you've just come back into the country, can be shocking. Though smaller in physical size than many suburban grocery stores, Fairway was so packed with product from floor to ceiling, aisle to aisle, front to back, that I wondered how any product could rise above the noise and attract a consumer's attention. Competing in this crowded market of products seemed impossible.

During my lifetime, the American consumer packaged goods industry had been on a tear, offering up thousands of new brands and products every month to appeal to every imaginable human need and desire. When I was a kid the average supermarket had around eight thousand different products on the shelves. Only a few decades later, the weekend shopper at the supermarket might now have to sort through upward of *forty thousand*. "Consumers have always had choices, but today options have exploded beyond all reason," said Barry Schwartz, author of *The Paradox of Choice*. "It's the ethos of American society; the idea that freedom is good, more is better, and you enhance those ideas by offering choice. Logically you can't hurt anyone by adding options. That's the theory, but in practicality it's not true."

But as I began to examine the offerings on the shelves, the challenge of creating a coconut water brand that would be noticed began to be less daunting. So many of the "new" offerings were simply spins and slight variations of old standards. A gallon of Breyers vanilla ice cream might take multiple forms: "Natural," "French," "No Sugar Added," "Extra Creamy," "Lactose-Free," and "Homemade." Then there were the thousands of look-alike and generic products that were simply mimicking category leaders. Companies were grabbing valuable shelf space (and bumping up their margins) but not really presenting consumers with anything truly unique.

These dynamics were particularly at play in the beverage aisle. The large amount of floor space allocated to beverages wasn't surprising given that the U.S. nonalcoholic packaged and fountain beverages industry generated over a quarter-trillion dollars in annual sales domestically. In 2005, that represented nearly 36 billion gallons in product annually or 121 gallons per person each year. Americans were drinking the equivalent of about four 12-ounce. cans of packaged beverage every single day. In the U.S., Coke's brands and product extensions accounted for around 40 percent of what was being sold. Pepsi, with a similar number of offerings, held about a third of the market, while Dr Pepper Snapple brands together (known as Cadbury Schweppes at the time) had about 15 percent. Every other company in the marketplace was way back in the pack, the largest in the low single digits.

Despite all those brands, all that shelf space, the huge financial resources, and hundreds of employees tasked with bringing new products to market, these big companies were doing a horrible job on the innovation front. At that time, only seven individual brands accounted for almost two-thirds of all sales: Coca-Cola Classic (itself with nearly 20 percent of the market), Diet Coke, Pepsi, Diet Pepsi, Mountain Dew (a Pepsi product), Sprite (a Coca-Cola product), and Dr Pepper. Nothing else came close. As for innovation, Coke and Pepsi had a long list of failures at launching new brands even after investing hundreds of millions of dollars and spending years of effort. New Coke, Fruitopia, Tab Clear, Josta, and Crystal Pepsi all failed to gain real momentum. Their relative successes were mostly derivative of other bestsellers: Sprite (1950s) was a 7UP knockoff, Powerade (1990s) followed Gatorade, and Dasani (1999 by Coke) and Aquafina (1994 by Pepsi) were knockoffs of the many bottled waters.

While Coke and Pepsi were category-leading brands and very well-run companies, outside of their core carbonated brands, they weren't having much success bringing anything truly new to market. This put them in a bind because by 2003, traditional soft drinks were falling from their high watermark. Even if soda sales declined by only 1 percent per year in the U.S., that meant the big dogs—Coke, Pepsi, Dr Pepper—would lose more than $300 million in sales. That also meant that every three years people were drinking $1 billion worth of something else, more when you account for population growth.

Industry experts were beginning to speculate that there would be $10 billion worth of beverage sales up for grabs in a decade if the decline of soda accelerated as expected.

Though not evident in the main fifty-foot beverage aisle with sodas, teas, waters, and sports drinks, another section of Fairway existed that was significantly different and much more interesting. At the front of the store was a six-foot-wide refrigerated section that offered individual bottles meant as grab-and-go purchases. This cooler was stocked with brands, a few of which I had heard of, including Red Bull and Snapple, but others that were new to me: Monster, Rockstar, and other energy drinks; and Izze, Jones Soda, GuS, and other interesting spins on carbonated soft drinks. There were also bottles of Honest Tea, Steaz tea, and Fuze; Smartwater, Volvic water, Nantucket Nectars, POM Wonderful, Odwalla, Naked Juice, and Muscle Milk. More than any other brand, Vitaminwater dominated the display with seven different brightly colored bottles.

Given the relatively small space available in that front-of-the-store refrigerator, it was hard to see these players as major competition to the legacy brands in the market. Then I reconsidered, as I witnessed half a dozen consumers step in and grab one or more bottles. Though buying one or two units at a time, their purchases were clearly adding up. In fifteen minutes I watched ten times the number of consumers take something from this shelf versus the main beverage aisle, which relied on purchases of multipacks, large jugs, and other volume formats. I also saw two restocking guys go to work in that time refilling the cooler from a cart loaded with cases of different brands. One of the guys, wearing a green smock, seemed like he worked for the store. The other was wearing a black Vitaminwater T-shirt. I asked him if he worked for Glacéau (I knew that was the parent company of the Vitaminwater brand). He said, *"Como?"* So I switched to Spanish. *"Tú trabajas para la empresa* Vitaminwater?"

"No," he said, "*para* Big Geyser, *la distribuidora.*" I made a mental note of that.

I couldn't find any coconut water in this cooler or in the main beverage aisle. That was good news. I did finally locate some in the ethnic aisle on the bottom shelf next to Cuban black beans and canned chili peppers, and there were three brands in tall, cheap-looking cans. Clearly, that wasn't the place for the brand I was imagining. No question I wanted to see my product someday in that front refrigerated case with the exciting new beverages. But I knew I had a lot to learn about how to get it on that shelf and stand out from the crowd.

Walking back to my hotel, I decided to take a peek at the shelves of a couple of little corner markets. The greater New York area has thousands of these small independently owned shops. One of the stores I walked into was filled with organic produce, fresh flowers, fine cheeses, and fresh baked bread. The beverage cooler, though smaller than the one at Fairway, had many of the same products. Clearly someone was buying these drinks, as I could only imagine what real estate cost in this neighborhood and I'm sure every inch of cooler space would be dedicated only to products that consistently sold at a high profit margin. I would later learn that for many of these bodega operators, the beverage "cold box" alone generated enough profit to cover their rent.

Compared to, say, making a car, barriers to entry for beverages are relatively low. (It's not a coincidence that setting up a lemonade stand is often a kid's first experience in running a business.) I would find out later that over three thousand new nonalcoholic beverages were launched every year. Most of these new brands didn't first appear in major retail outlets. They were being rolled out at farmers' markets, county fairs, and in small mom-and-pop stores across the country like the bodega I was in. This is where the innovation was happening in the beverage industry.

I shifted my attention from what was on the shelves to the customers doing the shopping. Given the markups in these small shops, I had a hard time imagining anyone filling up a shopping cart—in fact, shopping carts wouldn't fit down these narrow aisles. This was a place to get things on the go. Some of the shoppers were construction workers grabbing a beer at the end of the day. Others were business professionals buying a coffee, Coke, or water.

But there were also a number of consumers in their twenties, thirties, and forties who were different. They were groomed and stylish, in an understated sort of way. Though wearing distressed printed T-shirts and jeans that gave them the appearance of being down and out, their shoes gave them away. Here were the famed hipsters everyone was starting to talk about. Several women, I noticed, carried yoga mats under their arms, and many of the men were also clearly fresh from a workout. They were taking time to read labels and compare products, and I got the feeling that they were willing to spend money on quality food and drink. A couple bought some of the beverages that were new and different. I picked up a bottle of Fuze and while paying for it at the counter asked the clerk, "Does this sell well?"

"Yes, yes, sell good, sell good," he said in a strong Asian accent, not interested in talking to me.

"Who brings this to you?"

He said, "No time kwes-ton. Tree dollar, please. Many customer. You come later. A-na-der time. Aks kwes-ton. Bye bye."

I could have seen these entrepreneurial beverage brands in this small bodega as yet more competition, but I didn't really think of them in that way. Honestly, I was excited to join them. Simply from my introduction to these products, I imagined the people behind them must be interested in the same sort of objectives and mission. Yes, they were potential competitors, but they were also fellow seekers and their success to date offered proof of a growing desire in the marketplace for something different, new, and healthier. Little did I know most of them would not see it the same way and that it was virtually a cage match to the death to try to get and keep that valuable shelf space. That Korean shopkeeper's annoyance at my questions was my first clue. He was probably sick and tired of being quizzed by would-be entrepreneurs and pushy salesmen on an hourly basis. I later learned that these types of stores were on the front line of the new beverage wars and that this conflict was serious, brutal, and bloody. Any of the three thousand new beverages every year had about as much chance of surviving as any random high school senior getting into Harvard; in fact, less.

When I got back home to El Salvador, I began to devote my early mornings and evenings to reading everything I could find about recent trends and successes in the beverage industry. As I had gleaned from my on-the-ground research, innovation in nonalcoholic beverages was coming from outside corporate offices. If the big guys did have a successful new brand in their portfolio, it was almost always because they had purchased it from an entrepreneur who had brought it to life.

Further, the ranks of those successful beverage entrepreneurs came from a broad range of backgrounds rather than former industry professionals with an inside track. Indeed, students of innovation in all fields often conclude that being an outsider confers a big advantage: you're not constrained by the conventional wisdom about why a particular product or approach will or won't work.

WHO WILL YOU KICK OFF THE SHELF?

I had learned that retailers, distributors, and others in the industry would tend to think about what product ours would substitute: "Who are you going to kick off the shelf?" the saying goes. So I knew my first goal would be to define the beverage categories that coconut water might fall into and then research the winners and losers in each. That first part proved easier said than done. Those who analyzed the beverage industry generally broke down products into a half-dozen broad categories: carbonated soft drinks, juices, sports drinks, energy drinks, bottled water, and ready-to-drink teas. Some had defined a category being referred to as "New Age." These included herbal iced teas, specialty smoothies, some shelf-stable dairy drinks, and some nutritionally enhanced beverages. Others used the term "functional beverages" to describe drinks that claimed to provide a specific physiological benefit like hydration, increased energy, or wakefulness.

Interestingly, coconut water wasn't tracked at all in the industry numbers. Reliable data on the size of the market represented in the ethnic aisle was nearly impossible to find. I wondered how the beverage industry might categorize it once they decided to track it. I didn't want to put our brand next to those tall steel cans from brands like Goya or Foco anyway, with their low price point, added sugar, and preservatives. Clearly, coconut water wasn't a carbonated soda and it wasn't a tea. But how it fit into the other categories wasn't so obvious. I assumed coconut water was technically a juice. I also felt that because it had an exotic and cross-cultural appeal, it could work in the New Age category as well as offer an attractive alternative to bottled water. With all those electrolytes, it was certainly functional and could be seen by many consumers as a sports drink. I thought about the challenge of introducing U.S. consumers to something foreign and thought there was something to learn from alternative milks like soy. In the end, where would I suggest a store manager place our product on his shelves? I didn't have a clue.

One of my biggest learnings was that plenty of upstart winners in the beverage game were not experts when they launched. In fact, many were complete outsiders. For example, three New York City friends, two of them window washers and the third the owner of a small health food store, created Snapple. SoBe was created by John Bello, who'd had early stints at Pepsi and General Foods but had achieved his business success manufacturing and marketing jerseys, helmets, and other merchandise licensed by the National Football League. Bello decided to jump into this growing market with his own brand, South Beach, later restaged as SoBe.

This discovery led to another: that outsiders who venture into the beverage business could employ a ready network of companies positioned to help out the growing number of entrepreneurs. As with the hopeful forty-niners on the way to the gold fields, there are many companies ready to sell the modern-day beverage or food entrepreneur the tools and resources they'll need to succeed.

Flavor houses, from industry giant Wild Flavors to more boutique operations like Allen Flavors (AriZona Iced Tea's longtime flavor house), offered to help procure ingredients and get the flavor right. Packaging brokers like Zuckerman Honickman would procure bottles and cans for ventures that were too small to be worth the attention of big producers. Co-packers scattered around the country could work out the kinks and complete the first production runs. Distributors could test out new products and stick with the winners. These early experiments and help weren't cheap, so entrepreneurs needed financing up front, and often gave away equity in their companies as well, to get access to this insider network.

I came to understand that these suppliers, consultants, and middlemen companies were arguably the real success stories behind the new beverage bonanza. While they didn't make headlines or sell their companies for lottery-size winnings, these companies (and there are hundreds of them) are the true backbone of the beverage ecosystem that, for a price, help bold entrepreneurs bring their dreams to market.

This was particularly true of the distributors. Renowned independent distributor Big Geyser had helped put many brands on the map, including Nantucket Nectars, which then became one of the company's most important brands in its powerful network of independent route owners across the city. When Cadbury bought Nantucket Nectars, they pulled it from Big Geyser and gave it to their own Snapple distributors in New York. The Big Geyser team lost a big brand and in their fury looked for another one to get behind in a big way. They turned their attention to a small, fledgling brand they already had on their trucks: Vitaminwater. By the time I was walking the streets of New York, Big Geyser was already proving that, though often overlooked from the outside, the motivations of a distributor can make or break a brand.

THINKING OUTSIDE OF CATEGORIES

The industry focus on categories made for interesting reading, and I was learning the lay of the land, but partway through my research, I began to wonder whether these somewhat arbitrary lines between product groupings were really important. I also thought it might be one of the things hindering the major players in the industry from innovating successfully. As a consumer, I knew that I never once thought in terms of these categories when I bought a beverage.

So I decided to pursue this line of thinking instead of researching the industry further: what was *I* thinking when I made a purchase? When you are looking to understand the consumer marketplace, you always have one consumer ready to give you endless amounts of time: yourself. Because I didn't have the budget to conduct sophisticated or large-scale marketing tests, I decided to make a study of ourselves, which worked because I saw Maura and myself as target consumers for our coconut water brand. And it turns out that doing a deep dive on one consumer can tell you a good deal about an entire demographic.

Clearly the beverages I bought were about quenching thirst, but they were most often related to occasions or time periods in my day. I was looking for something to give me energy in the morning, to replenish and rehydrate me after a workout, or to give me a pick-me-up in the afternoon.

Remarkably, during my time in Central America coconut water had become my go-to drink during all those moments. It had pretty much replaced orange juice as my morning drink, especially as a base for the fruit smoothies Maura and I had almost daily. I drank it after a hike or swim instead of a sports drink in order to replenish, or in the middle of the afternoon to give me a boost of energy to get through the rest of the day. Plus, I found nothing was better to help my recovery after a rough night out on the town.

Of course, other, more intangible reasons determined why I picked one product over another. Many of those can be traced back to my particular generation and demographic group. Most sociologists would mark me as a vanguard Gen-Xer. My parents were undoubtedly influenced by trends that came from the activist 1950s Catholic community. They were dedicated to social justice, the women's movement, and racial harmony. These forces influenced them as consumers as well. The Rampolla household of the 1970s and 1980s was ahead of the cultural curve when it came to healthy, natural eating. I remember eating homemade granola, natural peanut butter, and preservative-free jam from the monastery on whole-wheat bread. Dad made buckwheat and buttermilk pancakes from scratch with a little wheat germ thrown in for good measure. The reality was that healthy eating was cheaper, too. Raising six kids on one salary meant giant pots of homemade soups and casseroles.

Although my family's eating habits were a little unusual in the working-class suburbs of Pittsburgh, I later realized that we were just slightly ahead of a major national trend. When I was a kid, the health food industry started to influence the public discussion about health and food in general, and it wasn't long before it was leading the conversation. Similarly, during my childhood, the first health food stores started to appear. In their early days, they appealed to a very narrow consumer group—the true countercultural hippies. They had wooden shelves and a few hundred products: fresh fruits and vegetables, bins of whole grains and cereals, handmade soaps, tofu and soy milk.

By the time I was out of college in the 1990s, exercising, eating healthy food, and avoiding highly processed products was no longer radical. It was mainstream. The juice and smoothie brands born in the 1980s, Odwalla and Naked, were clearly riding this cultural wave. The same was true for soy milk. When soy milk was launched in 1978, you could only find it in health food stores as a dairy substitute for the granola crowd. It took decades but the maturing of the health food market helped products like Silk to become billion-dollar brands. Honestly, I had hopes that coconut water wouldn't take as long to reach the mainstream, and I had good reason to be optimistic. After all, the new health food brands launching wouldn't have to change the country's attitudes about food and health, since a previous generation of health food entrepreneurs had already done that hard work for us.

The rise of the many companies in the once-ghettoized health food space was a remarkable and heartening achievement. For a hundred years, the beverage industry had made trillions of dollars playing only to a single innate human desire: sweetness. The taste for sugar is a powerful desire, but it is far from the only thing that people want or need. The major players failed to perceive other market demands. I realized that people, like me and our target consumers, want to have a long and healthy life. They want to know that what they put in their bodies will help them perform their best. They want to raise healthy children. They don't want their teeth to fall out before they're fifty. They want to maintain weight and fitness that suits their lifestyle. They want to look good and feel good, not just in the present moment but in the long term as well.

In creating endless variations on sugary drinks, legacy beverage companies not only failed to satisfy these other consumer desires, they actually made these other desires more salient and powerful. As the general population became less healthy—in part because of their addiction to sugary drinks—the demand grew around what was missing outside of sugary options. Meanwhile the health food sector had started gaining momentum and changing the public's attitudes and preferences. The health food market had done much in a generation, but the work was not yet done. It was time for a new generation of entrepreneurs to keep the momentum going.

TANKS A LOT

That day of prowling markets in Manhattan had me feeling overwhelmed at first, but by the time I left I felt excited and hopeful. Given that I wanted to provide something new and innovative, I might have to compete for shelf space but I wasn't competing against what was on the shelves. Upward of 95 percent of what was out there was a legacy brand, a copycat, or something that was narrowly derivative—and what I wanted to bring to market was entirely different.

Whether or not we'd be able to execute as well or better than some of the great beverage brands was a huge unknown. Coconut water might be unfamiliar to many Americans but it wasn't new to the world. We would do our best to make sure our coconut water was great tasting and nutritious, but we didn't own a coconut farm and didn't have a proprietary source or strain of coconut. The goal was also to keep the product to a single or very few ingredients: coconut water. We knew we'd have competition (little did we know that there would be a hundred coconut water brands in the U.S. alone within a decade), especially if we were successful, and we would constantly compete with all beverages for the so-called share of stomach.

Did the countless product failures make me nervous? Of course. I can't imagine who wouldn't be unnerved by the fact that only a small percentage of new beverage offerings ever break through to make any real money. This was a market that not even the brilliant Sir Richard Branson could succeed in. Only a few years before I began to consider launching a coconut water company, Sir Richard rode into Times Square on a tank to launch Virgin Cola. Despite being backed by one of the most successful entrepreneurs in history, good luck finding that brand anywhere today (well, maybe Tunisia). Big-budget launches were mostly flaming out, and thousands of little entrepreneurial offerings were popping up and dying out so fast, no one could really keep track.

Entering such a market was daunting. But I looked at all this activity in a more positive way. After my afternoon walking those cramped Fairway aisles, I realized that a crowded marketplace is also an information-rich one. I still had so much to learn, but with tens of thousands of other brands throughout history and thousands more coming online each year, I had plenty of case studies to learn from. If I did my homework, I didn't have to make their mistakes. No tanks for me. I couldn't afford to rent one and wouldn't know how to drive it even if I could.

CHAPTER 4
FINDING THE BRAND WITHIN YOU

As I started to think about creating a brand of coconut water, I studied one product closely: Vitaminwater. Everyone else in the industry was doing the same because it was taking the beverage market by storm. By 2003, industry analysts estimated the company had revenue approaching $100 million. Sales of the brand were rivaling Propel and even Gatorade in some markets, and it was growing by 30 percent per year in New York and more than 50 percent overall as it expanded to new markets. There was even talk about Vitaminwater becoming the next billion-dollar brand. Clearly, if I was going to be a player in this industry, I had to understand why they were so successful.

During that same business trip to New York in 2003, I bought a flavor of Vitaminwater called Revive and sat down on a park bench to take a look. Their bottle and packaging was designed to look pharmaceutical, which appealed to a consumer who wanted to look smart and educated but also tapped into some interesting American lore—the days of old-time apothecaries. (Kiehl's hits the same cultural note, to great success, in the personal care world.) I read the label, which had a catchy, sassy story: "HEY!! How's it goin? IS THIS TOO LOUD FOR YOU?? OH SORry? there. better? . . . we've all been there: last night's outfit doubled as last night's PJs . . . on days like these we recommend hydrating with this bottle."

I opened the bottle and took a sip. In terms of the drink itself—the ingredients, functionality, and taste—Vitaminwater was hardly an innovation. It was sweet and tasty but no more so than other products. What it did offer was a better story about itself at just the right moment in American culture, communicating a narrative of which consumers wanted to be a part.

J. Darius Bikoff, the brain behind Vitaminwater, had been messing around in the beverage industry for a few years by that time. He formed Energy Brands, Inc., in 1996 and launched his first brand, Go-Go energy drink, a female-focused beverage line. That brand struggled and was clearly too early (and perhaps too narrow with the female focus) for the energy drink boom, so Bikoff developed a premium water brand called Smartwater, under a parent company with the cool European-sounding name Glacéau (with meaningless accent mark, of course). Smartwater began to gain some traction in New York and the Northeast mainly in natural and specialty food stores, in part because Bikoff took cases in the trunk of his Mercedes door-to-door to retailers to gain shelf space. Glacéau then introduced Fruitwater, but it wasn't until 2000 when they introduced Vitaminwater that sales started to really take off.

The timing was perfect for something to bridge the soda and water gap, and Vitaminwater was catching the wave at just the right moment. Consumers were becoming aware that too much soda was not good for them and they were looking for a change. Bottled water was suddenly on the rise even though most of it was just tap water and it was a bit boring. In stepped Vitaminwater. It positioned itself as healthier than soda but better tasting than water. A little dose of vitamins and fun names like Detox and Revive made it clear when, how, and why to drink them. The company turned to a leading flavor house to develop tasty and creative concoctions using ginkgo biloba, green tea, pomegranate: all things consumers had sort of heard about, sort of believed in, but weren't sure how to use unless told how to do so. They tapped designer Philippe Starck to come up with a unique bottle shape and label design. They used bright, fun colors. They used natural flavors and real sugar (not high-fructose corn syrup).

The brand was designed to look authentic and smart, which was working well for Vitaminwater. The problem I saw was that it was mostly a fake message. As anyone who actually read the label would discover, Vitaminwater was basically sweetened, flavored water. Worse yet, they were capitalizing on an old trick in the beverage and snack industry: they served the stuff in 20-ounce bottles clearly designed for single use, but the requisite labeling showed that there were 2.5 servings in each container. So instead of getting the 13 grams of sugar stated on the label, you were getting 32.5 grams if you drank the whole bottle. That came to 125 calories, which is pretty near the 140 calories in a can of Coke. Oh, and that peppy feeling you got from the drink wasn't from the vitamins and minerals; it was the 150 milligrams of caffeine (at least in the Revive flavor)—the equivalent of two strong cups of espresso and almost *twice* the dose in a can of Red Bull.

The folks at Glacéau had to be assuming customers weren't going to read the label carefully. They also must have assumed that those who thought they were being smart and healthy would be so disconnected from the sensations and reactions of their own physiology that they wouldn't notice how bad they felt after the sugar and caffeine wore off. I came to learn that this cynical subterfuge was widely discussed. The brand was built on hype and misrepresentation. Those vitamins in the water? "Pixie dust" was what Maura would call the minute amounts each bottle contained.

I was certain that Vitaminwater was due for a consumer backlash but I was wrong about how long it would take and how high the brand would climb first. For four or five more years the brand continued to be a juggernaut. The people at Coke thought that the trend would continue and would scale across the world, because in 2007 they bought Glacéau for $4.1 billion, more than ten times its revenue at the time. Bikoff reportedly made close to $1 billion on the deal. By 2013, BevNET reported "sales of Vitaminwater are in the midst of sustained slide, pointing to a consumer that wants something else." (However, the sister brand, Smartwater, would more than make up for that loss.) In recent history, no other beverage brand achieved such massive success followed by such a stunning fall from grace as Vitaminwater (with perhaps Snapple under Quaker Oats's "stewardship" a close second).

The lesson for me was that if a brand could tell a compelling story, it could change behavior. Vitaminwater told a great story, was beautifully designed, chose the right early adopters and cultural influencers, and appealed to the health aspirations of a generation. But it wasn't authentic and it wasn't honest. Vitaminwater was proof that consumers were looking for a healthy alternative to soda. What would happen, I wondered, if we created a brand of coconut water with an equally compelling cultural positioning that was actually natural and healthy, and that told a story that matched the product and was truly authentic?

CRACKING THE RIGHT NUT

Despite having what might be a good idea, at the beginning of founding Zico (before it was even called Zico) I was hardly an insightful entrepreneur and really wasn't much of a marketer at all. My first impulse in bringing coconut water to America was to target the Hispanic market beginning in Los Angeles or Miami. That quickly growing demographic was all the talk among the consumer products industry at the time. So I thought I had struck gold when on a plane back from El Salvador my sister, Mary Beth, met Jose Gonzalez, former president of Publicis Sanchez & Levitan, a prominent Hispanic advertising agency that had developed a marketing strategy to help mainstream brands go after the Hispanic market. He and his friend and fellow Hispanic marketing expert Roberto Ruiz had recently started their own marketing agency, and I hired them to develop the brand positioning and marketing strategy for our coconut water.

After examining the thriving marketplace, however, Gonzalez and Ruiz gave me advice that wasn't what I expected. While Hispanics had more knowledge of coconut water as a beverage, they also had some solidly embedded cultural associations that would be hard to rewire. First of all, most Hispanics in the U.S. were now second generation. Since they were born and raised in the U.S., they had about as much firsthand experience with coconuts as I did growing up: next to none. For those who already liked coconut water and drank it regularly, they would gravitate toward the Hispanic brands they knew and could buy in specialty stores in the U.S. for a dollar. (I knew we'd need to charge much more than that for our higher-quality brand). For many others, the drink represented something that they had culturally moved on from—or something that only their parents or grandparents drank. Marketers had great success convincing young Latin American consumers that Heineken was cool, but that's because that brand had already become a cultural icon itself. Selling a partially known quantity like coconut water and a completely unknown brand would be much harder. Their conclusion: if I wanted to build a mainstream brand like I hoped to, don't target the Hispanic market first.

Gonzalez and Ruiz could have told me what they knew I wanted to hear, but thankfully they didn't. If I had tried to appeal to the American Hispanic market, it would likely have been a disaster. As much as I felt connected to Latin American culture, my knowledge only ran so deep. Even with Gonzalez and Ruiz's sage advice, I doubt I could have hit the right cultural note for this community that would overcome all these obstacles.

Who was I creating this brand for, then?

BRANDING WITH VALUES

Living abroad gives you fresh eyes on changes in your home culture. When Maura and I came back to the U.S. from Central America for visits in the early 2000s, we'd point out to each other the new trends and products that had surfaced in the time we'd been away. We began to notice products that suggested something new was going on in consumer culture—people were tiring of the mass produced, and the overly processed and artificial. We were, too.

Consumers were increasingly gravitating toward products with character—things that were from a specific place with interesting stories. Maura and I found Burt's Bees in the skincare product aisle, offering creams and ointments that defied the glamour- and youth-obsessed beauty product industry. These products had a personality and told a story of northeastern backwoods know-how and connection to nature. Like many families, we became devotees of the brand—trusting it enough to use on our girls. I don't remember seeing any advertisements for Burt's Bees but somehow it still communicated a sense of authenticity to us.

Burt's Bees wasn't alone in creating a brand that communicated purpose, passion, and values and gained our loyalty. Patagonia, which became a favorite of Maura and mine, fully embraced their customers' commitment to the environment. The whole ethos of the company, from the quality of its products to its commitment to the environment to its origin story, all spoke to an utterly different way of thinking about clothing and business. It was founded by Yvon Chouinard—the most unlikely of clothing moguls in the most unlikely of places: a backyard blacksmith shop. At heart a tinkerer and inventor, Chouinard created a brand that was an expression of his fresh and quirky view of the world and his love of wilderness adventure. It not only brought enthusiastic consumers but also informed the entire enterprise. His management style was new and counterintuitive, as evidenced by his book on the topic, *Let My People Go Surfing.*

The most exciting and successful brands are imbued with this sense of mission, personality, and personal values. More recently, Hampton Creek, which creates mayonnaise and other foods out of only plant-based ingredients, is taking the food industry by storm. Founder Josh Tetrick is a human- and animal-rights activist who is committed to remaking our food system to be free of animals. Thrive Market, founded by Gunnar Lovelace and Nick Green, is democratizing healthy food by bringing Whole Foods–quality products, with a Costco membership model and delivered like Amazon, to average consumers and so-called food deserts at low prices, so everyone has access to affordable healthy living.

These founders are clearly and honestly proud of their businesses; they were almost badges of honor not only in terms of the specific products but also in terms of the brands. Roxanne Quimby, behind Burt's Bees, was evangelical about the efficacy of all-natural products. Tetrick takes out *Wall Street Journal* ads encouraging young entrepreneurs to compete with him to offer more plant-based foods. Thrive Market gives away one free membership to a low-income family for every one they sell. These entrepreneurs are on a personal quest not just to get rich, but also to change culture and to try to make the world a better place.

All of these brands have something to teach the new entrepreneur but none of them are possible to mimic. They are as individual and unique as a great piece of art—their uniqueness is what creates their authentic feel. You can look to these successes for inspiration but you can't look to them to find the thing that you have to offer.

I didn't have a particular set of traditional skills to begin with but nevertheless, I still wanted to display that same pride of ownership and personal connection to whatever we created. I wanted my brand to be a badge of honor: for me, our family, our eventual team, producers and suppliers, and consumers.

In thinking about how to create an authentic brand, our only hope was to employ the same logic that got us to the idea of coconut water in the first place. It had to be a brand that appealed to Maura and me first and foremost. We had a commitment to our personal health, and the health of others and the environment. We led active lifestyles and loved adventure. We aspired to live a long, interesting, and healthy life and see the world become a better place for the next generation. We liked to have fun, party, and let loose. I assumed there were millions of people that were very much like us. But thinking about a group that large was an abstraction. I realized our best chance of creating something authentic was if we focused on the values and drive behind the idea, and kept ourselves, the people closest to us, and our hopes, values, and desires in mind at every turn.

SEED CAPITAL

In my research of successful upstart brands in the beverage industry, I learned that they all needed money: lots of it. Some years earlier, SoBe had supposedly built its brand for under $8 million in total capital raised. By 2004, Glacéau seemed to be raising that amount of investment every few months. Maura and I certainly were not going to finance anything close to that ourselves. We were going to need plenty of OPM—other people's money—and need it fast, before we took any further steps.

By the second half of 2003, I had done enough research and had enough confidence to begin telling people about our big idea. Up to that point, I had kept the concept just between Maura, Mary Beth, and me. Many entrepreneurs stay stuck in this spot for too long, guarded about talking about their idea for fear of someone stealing their brilliance. The downside to trying to protect your idea from being copied, however, is that you miss out on learning from people who can help in critical and sometimes surprising ways.

My approach was to talk about my idea to anyone with ears. In retrospect, I see how this approach helped me avoid many pitfalls, allowed me to make critical adjustments early, and maximized the serendipitous good luck that was crucial to our success. The truth is, you don't know where the most help will come from. The guy sitting next to you at the hotel bar might be a hungry young executive of a distribution company, a successful serial entrepreneur, a venture capital bigwig, or have a good friend who is a buyer for Whole Foods. Talking to literally everyone about your idea increases the odds you'll experience that magical moment where someone says, "Interesting, I actually know someone you should talk to . . ."

And that's exactly how I found all of our earliest investors. I wasn't just looking for those willing to write a check; I wanted investors who believed in me and the project, who shared my values and could add knowledge, insight, and connections. Finding these types is not easy but by telling my story to anyone and everyone, they started to appear.

I was fortunate that my International Paper job had brought me into personal contact with many Central American businesspeople. Over a business dinner, I laid out the idea to two of my top customers in my day job, Mario Carvajal and Hernan Bravo. Hernan had been a marketing executive for Coca-Cola in Central America, and together he and Mario owned and operated a beverage company that owned a brand called Kapo, which they distributed through Coca-Cola Central America. I would typically never discuss something like this with customers but we had become close friends. I admired them, wanted their advice, and never directly asked them to invest. They both loved the idea of coconut water and had a barrage of difficult questions about how I would go to market. Before dinner was over Mario said he wanted to invest. Hernan was helpful with advice and was interested in investing but wanted to see more before he would commit.

At the end of the dinner, Mario wanted to know how committed I was. What would I do, he asked, if IP gave me a big promotion while I was still getting the business off the ground? "I'd turn them down," I replied. It was a prescient question. In the next year, I would be offered two substantial promotions, one in Brazil and the other in Belgium. I was far from certain this coconut thing would work out, but I believed in it enough to turn both of them down.

Next, I talked about the idea with the minority partners that were on my board of directors for International Paper El Salvador: Ricardo and Joaquin Palomo, Carlos Patricio and Francisco Escobar Thompson, and Pedro Apostolo. At Ricardo's birthday party the previous year, they all gathered around me and Maura and said they knew I would leave IP someday and start something on my own, and whatever it was, they wanted to invest. Now that their prediction had come true, I told them I was not expecting them to invest but wanted to give them the chance to follow through on that offer. They were true to their word.

I found two other critical early investors very close to me. My sister, Mary Beth, and my college friend Mike Lorenz both saw I was passionate about this idea when I talked to them about it. Though they didn't know anything about beverages specifically, both were savvy and successful businesspeople in their own right. I never asked them to invest and in fact discouraged it. I didn't want to put anyone close to me in the position of worrying that they might be letting me down by not investing. Mary Beth and Mike both told me they knew there were risks but believed in me, liked the idea, and wanted to invest.

Over the entire trajectory of Zico, and after raising tens of millions of dollars, my experience was that my best success in raising money was *not* to ask people for money, at least not directly. I would simply tell my story, believing I was giving everyone a great opportunity, and anyone who was even a potential investor would inevitably ask if we were raising money, which would open up the conversation. If they didn't ask, they were probably not a sophisticated enough investor to be making this sort of bet anyway or perhaps not the right fit. All of my investors knew and accepted they could lose (and could afford to lose) all of the money they offered. If you feel an investor can't, you don't want them.

For those with whom I had a deep personal connection, keeping the relationship intact was—for all parties—vastly more valuable than the money on the table, but at the same time no one likes to lose money. Taking money from "friends and family" is a mixed bag. If everyone goes in eyes wide open and the financial component is clear, well documented, and the risks accepted by all, then friends and family capital can be a critical and important place to start. If not, it's bad news, and I've seen it split families down the middle. Having Mary Beth, Mike, and eventually other friends, my own parents, other siblings, and even my mother-in-law as investors provided an additional layer of personal motivation for me: I did not want to let them down and deal with the resulting tension at holiday dinners.

SPROUTING THE ZICO BRAND

Now that I had commitments for at least some capital, it was time to dive in. We had a lot to do, including refining the business plan; determining the growers, processor, and distributors; deciding when and how to launch; planning and figuring out the right sales and marketing tactics; and building the right team. But first, we needed to build the foundations of our brand. We decided to start with the brand vision architecture: a single graphic that captures in as few words as possible what the brand is about and who it's for. Second, I knew we needed to get the right brand name. Third, we had to nail the visual branding: the look and feel of everything from T-shirts and hats to our website to point-of-sale displays, but especially the packaging itself. I believed these three elements would form the foundation of a great brand and the basis for the best and most authentic representation of what we wanted that brand to stand for.

Between Maura, Mary Beth, Jose, Roberto, and me, I was confident we had the right team to nail these three. To give the team direction, I created a sort of mini-manifesto, a one-page statement written in simple, clear, but passionate language outlining what our mission was, why we were doing this, and what we were all about. I wanted to make sure that everyone on the core team understood what I thought the brand should stand for before heading off to tackle these three first branding elements.

The brief reiterated the core mission: In twenty years, we wanted to see kids drinking coconut water, regardless of the brand, instead of high-sugar, artificial beverages, as part of leading healthier, more active lives. We hoped to catalyze economic growth in developing countries so tens of thousands of people could benefit from well-paying jobs in a healthy, sustainable, and growing coconut industry. Our brand would stand for healthy, natural, active living. Everyone involved with our company would have the opportunity to earn, learn, contribute, and grow to their fullest potential. The story we told about the product through the branding needed to honestly match the natural ingredients in the product. It would be a brand designed to have a long-standing and meaningful role in a cultural revolution in health and wellness.

After some back and forth, we came up with the image of a house, with the foundation representing "refreshment" and "replenishment," general attributes that any consumer would expect and the fundamental reason to drink coconut water. Next were three house pillars: "naturally pure," "unexpectedly healthy," and "authentically original," meant to describe both the physical and emotional attributes of our coconut water. The roof of the house was that the brand was "amazingly balanced." Not only was coconut water a well-balanced beverage readily absorbed by the body, but we also felt the brand should reflect living life in balance: finding the medium between the physical and spiritual, mental and emotional, family and business, doing and being. Both Maura and I loved this brand vision and knew it was consistent with our values and was something we wanted to be associated with and promote.

What's in a Name?

The next step in the process was coming up with the right name. We wanted a simple, bold, and memorable name. We wanted it to reference coconuts but be unique enough that we could create the meaning. If the whole word "coconut" was in the name, then consumers would bring their preexisting cultural meanings to the product. We wanted to tell our own story.

Mary Beth took the lead. She created a spreadsheet listing all the adjectives that we thought the name could elicit: pure, authentic, fresh, tropical, hydrating, replenishing, and more. We decided that one option was to include the syllable "co" of coconut in the name, so Mary Beth and her team began putting together a list of every possible two- or three-letter combination that might match that criteria and was catchy or graphically interesting: kico, soco, zoco, cozo, on and on.

Because we wanted our brand to have global potential, we checked our short list with people who knew other languages. You have to be fully fluent in another language to pick up on linguistic landmines, like the famous Chevy Nova, which, not surprisingly, fared poorly in Latin America. Who wants to buy a car that *"no va"* or "doesn't go"?

We had English covered and mostly Spanish but we wanted to make sure in Mandarin, Cantonese, Hindi, Arabic, Portuguese, Japanese, Italian, French, and German we weren't insulting someone's grandmother or worse. After that, Jose and Roberto set up small focus groups in New York to make sure that the connotations of the name were the ones we intended, or at least were neutral.

Next up was a legal review. So few names are available. Even when products are not on the market, lawyers and others have taken to "squatting" on names, claiming to be planning on launching a brand while actually only hoping to sell the name.

Finally, Mary Beth did a rough mock-up of how each name on our shortlist might look graphically and on the packaging to make sure we were comfortable with how it would read.

In the end, we narrowed it down to Vida and Zico. I'd love to tell you I chose Zico, but I was leaning toward Vida ("life" in Spanish). With Mary Beth, Jose, and Roberto all pushing me, I caved and went with Zico. Plus at this time, a "coming soon" website showed up online for another coconut water brand: Vita Coco. Vida would just be too similar. Another stroke of luck came when our publicist, Jon Osmundsen, called me and said, "Mark, isn't one of the names you're considering Zico? I just saw that the URL www.zico.com is for sale on eBay." Roberto waited until the bidding period was just about over and bought it for a thousand dollars.

Zico was a simple word and had an appealing look, especially in all capital letters. It meant nothing and was non-offensive in all major world languages as far as we could determine. The fact that the word wasn't descriptive—if you just saw the word, you wouldn't have a clue what the product was—we saw as an advantage. We were making a cultural play, not a strictly functional one. This would allow us to build the meaning behind the word ourselves. I always loved the letter "Z" for some reason and the "K" sound clearly had a strong track record with brands such as Coca-Cola, Kleenex, Clorox, Cartier, Cadillac, Spanx, to name a few.

We also thought it would be an advantage that people wouldn't immediately know how to pronounce the word. Part of the branding and marketing would have to teach consumers that it was "Zee-co" not "Z-eye-co." Correct pronunciation would delineate the consumers in the know. I felt like such a loser the first time I learned as a kid that the brand was "N-eye-k-ee" not "N-eye-k," but sure felt cool when I could point out the correct pronunciation to even less in-the-know friends.

Over the years, people have asked to learn the significance behind the name Zico. My answer—that we made it up—is always a little disappointing. But at the same time, that gave us a blank canvas that was an opportunity to create something new and hopefully disruptive. You don't want to limit your brand by picking a name with no flexibility or one that has only momentary cultural resonance. As long as you pick something unique and memorable that you can trademark in your space (and hopefully others) and that you won't tire of, you should be fine.

Design by Nature

Coconut water brought a lot of visual imagery to work with for packaging: the coconut itself, palm trees, beaches, a blue ocean, and pretty much every other tropical image imaginable. Unfortunately, many of these images were clichés that would need a great graphic designer to create something that looked new and not just a riff on Corona Extra beer. Thankfully, my sister Mary Beth, an architect and designer, had some serious cred in the design world, such as designing the corporate offices for mega-advertising firm Ogilvy & Mather.

Mary Beth and I always had a special bond. She was seven years older than me and protected me (most of the time) from our older brothers' fury, and as payback I let her girlfriends dress me up. (I'd have done just about anything to be around her beautiful friends.) Later, she taught me the important things in life, like how to sneak your own booze into a concert to avoid the lines and the proper etiquette for doing tequila shots. Though she had never designed a beverage package before, I trusted her more than the dozens of packaging designers I knew from working with customers at International Paper, who all seemed to do the same conventional packages with minor tweaks. I wanted something bold, something unique, and I couldn't imagine anyone better to do that than Mary Beth.

Mary Beth showed us what she had come up with when she visited us in El Salvador in 2003. On our dining room table, she set out a dozen Tetra Pak 330-milliliter Prisma packages with various versions of what the product might look like (we knew by then this package was the best available at the time to keep coconut water in a natural state, with no additives or preservatives). The prototype containers that Mary Beth had created represented a whole spectrum of ideas ranging from urban tough with gang tattoos to Brazilian Carnival to relaxing blue sky, palm trees, and coconuts. We looked at the choices and discussed who the imaginary customer might be and what we wanted to tell them—a commodity story or one of aspiration? If you are selling a commodity, like orange juice, the best thing to do is to put a big beautiful orange on the label. If you are selling an aspiration, you can be a lot more creative in your visual branding.

I told Mary Beth that I imagined Maura and myself as the key consumers. "Okay," Mary Beth said, "so we're looking at the twenty-five to forty-year-old age group. People who are active and healthy and want to keep that up. People with disposable income."

"Right," I said. "Except maybe for that last part. Disposable income is not something we had, or most people do, at twenty-five."

"Then I think we're looking for visual images that are more about aspirations," she concluded.

Two package designs were both simpler and cleaner than the rest. One was green with a reference to the classic yin and yang symbol. The other leveraged the beautiful deep blue of a tropical sky over the lighter blue of the ocean, with the deep green of a single palm tree at the top and the palm's distinctive shadow at the bottom. The Zico name ran vertically along the left side in all caps in a simple bold font that Mary Beth had created herself. I was leaning toward the green one because I felt green resonated with environmentally conscious consumers. Maura loved the simplicity and clarity of the blue one, though she wasn't crazy about the palm tree since anything remotely tropical usually had palm trees all over it. Adamant about the power of minimalism, Mary Beth then captured the essence of the brand by removing the image of the tree and leaving only its shadow.

A month later, when I was visiting Mary Beth in Chicago, we took mock-ups of the two packages to a local supermarket not far from her home late at night. We put all the mock Zico containers in a shopping cart and waited near the beverage aisle until we were alone. As fast as we could, we pulled other products off the shelves and replaced them with Zico containers. (If anyone was watching the security cameras, they were too puzzled or amused to sound the alarm.) We wanted to see exactly what our product would look like on actual store shelves.

I had to admit the blue ones stood out on the shelf much better—you could readily identify the brand from fifty feet away. But I still thought both packages were viable. It wasn't until a few months later in a small New York City usage test that my final decision was made. When a beautiful young Indian student at New York University was asked what she thought of the product and the two packaging options, she immediately picked up the blue one and said, "This one is beautiful, it reminds me of a beach back in India but I think it's modern and cool, I can totally imagine hanging with my friends, carrying it around and saying, 'I got my Zico, you got your Zico?'" Blue it would be.

Be the Brand

Creating a culturally innovative brand that is driven by your personal values and communicates authenticity to today's savvy consumers is easier said than done. It's easy to get off track at every step along the way, to forget your reason for starting, or to drift away from your values and early mission. When finances run low and things get scary, you can easily lose confidence. You begin to think: *What's the easiest way to appeal to the largest consumer market?* I'm not necessarily saying that focusing on such a question might not be the right way to go. And indeed, you may make a lot of money doing so, but you won't have a unique, impactful, potentially enduring brand that stands out because it represents your singular, personal vision, values, and contribution to the world.

CHAPTER 5
IT WILL NOT BE
THIS WAY

Just over a year after we had decided that coconut water was our
big idea, I flew with Maura to New York in June 2004 to introduce
Zico to the world at the Fancy Food Show. The annual show featured
over 180,000 products from 2,400 exhibitors targeting gourmet,
health, and specialty food and beverage distributors and retailers. As
best we could tell, no other coconut water had yet signed up for the
show, so we would be the first and hopefully only. But how, we wondered, could our new little brand get noticed among all the others?

On the plane, Maura and I talked about the coming few days. A
pallet with 250 cases of the first commercial production of Zico was—
hopefully—waiting at the Jacob K. Javits Convention Center along
with the makings of a new exhibit booth, boxes of branded T-shirts,
hats, beach balls, and more that Mary Beth designed to create a larger-
than-life Zico experience at the show.

We had accomplished an incredible amount in a short period of
time leading up to the Fancy Food Show, and I believed we were well
positioned to successfully launch Zico. I had also learned a ton

personally and thought I was finally ready to be an entrepreneur. As a couple, that period pushed our marriage as close to the brink as we had ever been and I hoped ever would be. I didn't think it could get any more intense. I figured if the show went well and I could quit IP and focus on Zico full-time, life would be a breeze, and I took to telling Maura, "This is as tough as it will get." I would soon find out what tough really meant.

The lights came on, that little bell rang, and the captain told us we were descending into New York. Tomorrow was our chance to see if this Zico thing was for real or not.

OUT ON A LIMB

Just four months earlier, in March of 2004, we had learned about the Fancy Food Show scheduled for that June. It was the perfect time and place to launch, except for two problems.

First, we didn't have the $50,000 in the business that we estimated it would cost to launch it right, including to: run a minimum production quantity (even though we only needed fifty cases for the show, we would have to produce at least two thousand at a time), rent and build the booth, travel, make T-shirts, hats, business cards, and more. Most of the early investors had verbally said they would invest more if the business plan looked viable and the terms acceptable. We were set to meet in April to review the full plan but this decision on the trade show couldn't wait until then. We had the money personally, but just a few months earlier I had drained our personal bank account to pay for the design and marketing research and the legal and other fees, and barely got reimbursed by our first investors in time to cover Christmas expenses with Maura's family in town.

The bigger problem was we didn't have any product to show. And we weren't close to having it: We didn't have coconut growers or processors, or packaging or even the final design. We had only ninety days to figure those pieces out and then convince everyone involved to get it done on a short timeline. There was still a massive amount of work to do and real uncertainty that we could make it happen in time.

As Facebook founder and CEO Mark Zuckerberg said, "The biggest risk is not taking any risk . . . In a world that's changing really quickly, the only strategy that is guaranteed to fail is not taking risks." So instead of waiting another four months for the next show or making sure I had money in the Zico bank account, we committed to the trade show and started the wheels in motion to get everything we needed. What's the worst that could happen? Our bank account would be back down to zero and we'd take a trip to New York and sit in a beautiful booth with no product to sample? That didn't sound so bad. Plus, we were on a mission now and nothing could hold us back.

IT'S WHAT IS ON THE INSIDE THAT COUNTS

With Zico, we wanted to create something that captured as close as possible the experience of drinking out of a freshly open young coconut. The problem, I quickly realized, was determing what type of coconut? From what country? The taste profile and nutritional properties could vary dramatically among the dozens of varieties available in the eighty-five tropical countries around the world that grow coconuts. How would we determine which was best?

A few months earlier while researching online, I came across Professor Charles Sims, an expert in the University of Florida's Food Science and Human Nutrition department (ironically the same university that developed Gatorade). Professor Sims specialized in understanding what production factors influence the sensory characteristics of fruits and vegetables. Since coconut water wasn't on the scene yet,

Sims didn't have all the answers, but he was happy to help define the right questions.

On the phone, he peppered me with questions about what characteristics we were looking for, like taste or nutritional content; what country had coconuts that met those requirements; and what scale of production we would need. Were there issues about the sustainability of coconut production? What would be the best packaging for coconut water? Would it need to be pasteurized? My head was spinning with all these questions so I decided to fly to Gainesville to meet with him in person. His team of researchers and I brainstormed how to approach these questions and roughed out a series of experiments to help us get answers. I had a few dozen varieties of coconuts of varying maturities from different countries sent to their lab (customs officials seem to be more tolerant of produce shipped to university labs). In addition, I shipped him every coconut water product from every overseas producer we could get ahold of. Sims and his team did a series of nutritional, sensory, and other tests on the products and then rounded up a roomful of students from different ethnic backgrounds (primarily Hispanic, Caribbean, and Caucasian) for taste tests.

What we learned was that though the Hispanic and Caribbean students were familiar with coconut water and had a positive association with it, they thought the pure, plain coconut water was not sweet enough. We came to understand, like Ruiz and Gonzalez had speculated, that though this demographic in the U.S. had heard tales of coconut water's benefits from parents and grandparents, most had only tasted the canned coconut water with added sugar, if anything. I knew from my beverage packaging days that most beverages in Latin America have more added sugar than in the U.S. (Even packaged coffee in Costa Rica sold for the local market at the time often had 10 percent added sugar.) Most of the Caucasian students were not familiar with coconut water at all, expected it to be milky, and often didn't like the taste. I fundamentally disagreed with adding sugar but thought adding natural juice or other familiar flavors might enhance the off taste of the plain coconut water. As best we could tell, no one in the world had brought flavored coconut water to market. Our Salvadoran friends thought this was sacrilegious: you didn't mess with coconut water. But it seemed obvious to me that we could use natural flavors or a small amount of juice as a way to overcome a taste profile that many Americans would likely not enjoy.

The most important learning was the level of inconsistency between the sources and even from batch to batch. The level of pH (acidity), brix (natural sugars), color, and other measures were significantly different from country to country and producer to producer, and even from batch to batch for some producers. For one of the main viable producers from Brazil, the conclusion of the University of Florida team was that given the level of difference between batches, they couldn't draw any conclusions at all. That was scary. Another supplier from Brazil, Amacoco, had the most consistent taste and nutritional profile and a higher taste appeal than the others. Professor Sims and his team also validated my assumption, after years of working with beverage packaging, that by using specialized processing and packaging, we could capture a taste much closer to fresh coconut water than canning or bottling and do so without adding sugar or preservatives.

No matter what type of coconut water we picked, however, I had to face the fact that a large percentage of consumers wouldn't like it on the first try. The *Onion* would have fun with that hard fact a few years later with the headline: "President Obama puts the U.S. economy in the hands of the geniuses behind Zico coconut water, who must know what they're doing because they are bringing in millions on a product that tastes like ass."

I prefer to say that for some people, coconut water in its plain, unadulterated state is an acquired taste, but call it what you will—we had a taste challenge on our hands. Coconut water is just so different from most beverages American consumers drink, which are highly sweet and tartly acidic. That combination, I learned, creates a particular sensation in the mouth, and we have grown used to it. Coconut water has a sort of smooth taste sensation, which comes mainly from the fact that its acidity level is so low: it doesn't have that acidic bite of most beverages.

We knew we weren't the first to face this challenge. The natural foods industry is full of products that take some learning to love but deliver a functional benefit: think kale, soy milk, or kombucha. The central claim for all these products isn't taste; it's *functionality*. The off-putting taste could be a selling point—as a "if it tastes that bad, it must be good for me" sort of logic.

We had no question that our main product would be 100 percent pure coconut water. We knew some consumers would know it and love it and want it unadulterated. But launching with that product alone had a major downside. We might never get a second try with some people and could turn off millions of potential consumers. Red Bull may have gotten away with only having one flavor for their first twenty years, but I believed we needed a different approach. We figured we'd need to come up with two or three natural flavor blends that would appeal to a wider audience and help introduce people who weren't wild about the taste of plain coconut water to its benefits.

The process started with us mixing at-home concoctions of coconut water with guava, lychee, star fruit, passion fruit, hibiscus, and some of the more exotic fruit available in Salvadoran markets. Our operations consultant Juan Carlos Rojas then guided us through the process of figuring out how to safely and cost effectively do this on an industrial scale once we decided where we would produce. In late March, Maura, Mary Beth, Juan Carlos, and I flew to Mexico to tour the facilities of Firmenich, a Swiss global ingredient and flavor company, to conduct taste testing on potential mixtures. By the end of our second day, we had narrowed it down to three flavors we thought were winners: mango, passion fruit–orange peel, and lemon-lime.

PLANTING A GLOBAL SUPPLY CHAIN

Figuring out where and how we were going to source coconut water was our next big step. Eighty-five countries grew coconuts. The U.S. (with small-scale exceptions in Hawaii and Florida) and Europe weren't among them, of course, which meant we'd be building a supply chain in some of the most challenging business environments in the world. I had personally witnessed International Paper, a major multinational with teams of lawyers, advisers, and experts, lose millions of dollars in the currency crisis of Brazil, the economic meltdown of Argentina, and the political crisis in Venezuela. One of the main territories for coconut production in the Philippines was so dangerous that I learned my life insurance policy wouldn't pay out if I died while traveling there.

Because of already established markets in the U.S. for coconut meat and oil, supply chains existed that we could learn from. As I had learned earlier, the water inside coconuts was often just a waste product in these manufacturing processes. Getting the water seemed easy until I learned that in many countries the farmers opened the coconuts at the farm and let the water drain right there on the ground to lighten their shipment of the more valuable coconut meat to the factories. Others grew coconuts to a maturity perfect for meat or oil but less ideal for water. I had heard rumors of one factory in Asia that processed one million coconuts per day for the meat, meanwhile letting the water run down the drain. That alone could supply a $200 million annual coconut water business! Research articles suggested dozens of extraction and processing techniques for the water, but there were very few producers in the world with the equipment and experience to actually do it—which was bad news, but also meant narrowing my search some.

I also realized we would have to make a series of decisions and potential trade-offs. For example, which was more important: higher electrolyte content of the coconut water or taste? We also had to figure out how we'd control for quality and consistency from batch to batch, season to season, and year to year. How could we ensure our supply chain had minimal environmental impact and maximum positive social impact? What were the trade-offs of sourcing from small farmers or cooperatives where we could perhaps establish a direct connection with them and support their development versus working with larger companies that had more resources and know-how? None of these questions had easy answers and I would struggle with many of them for most of the next decade. My goal in every case was to find the answer that was both best for the viability of the business and the one that represented our values. That solution was often available, but it was rarely obvious or easy to find.

We quickly concluded that our "backyard," Central America, was too small in coconut production and that the infrastructure was not developed enough. Most countries in Asia were geared toward meeting huge production for coconut meat and oil, and we believed it might be tough to switch them toward water right away other than low-quality canned coconut water.

Brazil showed promise. Though much smaller in total coconut production than Indonesia and the Philippines, Brazil's production was large enough to support huge growth. The major players there already had experience, and the total market in Brazil for packaged coconut water was over $30 million at that time, from zero just a few years earlier. That made it the largest market for higher-quality young coconut water in the world at the time. I was comfortable with the culture in Brazil, sort of knew the language, and had at least a few connections. Brazil had another advantage. Their currency, the real, was weak versus the U.S. dollar at the time, making it favorable to buy there. I couldn't know if that exchange rate would stay advantageous over time (it wouldn't) but at least in the short run it looked like a big advantage. Also, though Brazil was a large and fast-growing country, it had a large rural poor population, and the additional agricultural investment and growth was needed and welcomed to help the country develop further.

So we were off to Brazil, to meet personally with the two potential suppliers that we had learned about and tested at the University of Florida.

The Samba Supply Dance

At the time there were no "fair trade" or "organic" or other eco-certified coconut producers in Brazil, or in other countries for that matter. We'd have to design our own quality, social, and environmental audits. So before visiting Brazil, Juan Carlos and I worked up our agenda to find out as much as we could: We wanted to tour the plants and meet the quality assurance and production teams, the plant manager, and the head of human resources. We also wanted to go to the plantations to see where and how the coconuts were grown and harvested.

Brazil is almost as big as the U.S., and is a world away from little Central America. Juan Carlos flew from Costa Rica and I from San Salvador, arriving into Belém, a city of 1.5 million people, in the north of Brazil where Amacoco was based. The morning after we arrived, we were driven to the plant and had a sit-down meeting with the general manager, the head of export, and the plant manager. During that day, we met with the quality control manager, head of human resources, and various scientists and agronomists on their staff. We spent hours grilling the plant manager and quality control personnel about every step of their process. How often did they sample and test their product? Did they do it in-house or have outside auditors? I took it as a positive sign that the plant manager would leave us alone for discussions with his key staff members. At lunch we were given permission to dine in the company cafeteria along with the rank-and-file workers. Another good sign.

We learned that the lowest-level employees received a starting pay significantly above the minimum wage and what locally was a livable wage. Most of the jobs, however, required technical skills and were paid well above that. Just as important, the company kept close track of inflation rates and costs of basic-living goods and services in town so they could adjust wages in relationship with the sometimes erratic inflation rates. In addition, all employees shared in a bonus pool based on company profits. Other programs impressed me as well, such as the scholarship program they had for kids of employees to help them finish high school and attend college.

The next day Gerardo Lara, the plantation manager, picked us up at our hotel. On our drive to the company plantation, he told us how they had been growing coconuts on several thousand acres for twenty years and that it had likely been cattle pasture for decades before that. "And rain forest before that?" I asked. Likely so, he admitted, but that was probably over a hundred years ago. He said we would see a number of sections of the farm that they were reforesting. I certainly wanted to make sure no virgin or even secondary rain forest was cut to produce Zico, and that was clearly not the case.

When we arrived at his small office on the plantation, Lara showed us an aerial photo of the land on a wall. In the image I could see the distinctive tops of coconut trees in perfect rows separated by wide, dense green swaths in between. Lara said these were reforested biological corridors some one hundred to two hundred meters wide to allow wildlife to migrate between forested areas. Zoologists from a local university who studied the land, he said, had measured an increasing presence of wildlife every year, especially native birds, which he was particularly happy about because they helped naturally control bug populations that could harm his crops. Water came from a small tributary from the Guamá River and was diverted throughout the plantation. A local environmental organization measured water quality when it came onto the property and when it ran back into the river and discovered that it was often cleaner after than before. He gave us copies of several published studies and reports to back up his claims. When we asked about safety training we were shown the accident log, which didn't have a report of a major incident in the past year.

In the afternoon, we walked the property with an agronomist who told us all about coconut trees. Coconut palms, depending on variety, take three to five years to begin to produce usable fruit. At that point, they can yield upward of one hundred coconuts per year and remain productive for fifteen to twenty years. With each coconut producing roughly 330 milliliters of water, each tree could give 30 liters, or 8 gallons, per year for decades. To avoid potential plagues that can decimate monocultural crops, they planted a half-dozen different varieties on the property. They also were experimenting with mixing in banana plants, plantains, sugar cane, and other crops in the same area.

I had worried on the flight that no producer would meet the quality, environmental, and social standards we hoped for. But what we found were professional operators doing much more on each of these fronts than I ever expected, and in fact a better job than I probably could have done with $10 million and ten years to get it done. They were also surprisingly transparent and the sort of partners with whom I wanted to work.

Make It Personal

The following morning, while Juan Carlos stayed on to work with the plant manager on production details, I flew 2,000 kilometers to the south to Belo Horizonte to meet Luis Otavio, one of the main owners of Amacoco. Otavio didn't usually meet with prospective clients, but I worked every connection I had to get an audience. When I arrived at his beautiful old plantation-style home, it was clear that Luis was a very wealthy man. During lunch on a large veranda with Jeronymo, one of his key deputies, I told him of my impressions of his factory and factory farm.

I asked him about his vision for his coconut water business. He said he worried that Brazilian kids were adopting the U.S. preference of high-sugar sodas and sports drinks. He hoped to change that in Brazil and the rest of the world while providing good jobs and development to rural areas of the country—a familiar-sounding message. Coconuts were also very sustainable, he believed. Jeronymo jumped into the conversation to tell me that they had researched launching in the U.S. themselves but, without a clear plan to crack the market, had abandoned the project. He revealed that they'd recently been approached by other U.S. brands looking for a supplier. Had I ever heard of a company called Vita Coco? I nodded my head to indicate, *Of course, know all about them*, while the fact was I was desperate for information about this nascent competitor. All I knew of Vita Coco to that point was still the "coming soon" website.

"So they've approached you as well?" I asked offhandedly. "What was your impression?"

Jeronymo said they were young and not particularly knowledgeable but very aggressive and confident. He said Amacoco would sell to both us and them, unless one was willing to step up and make a major commitment.

Mentally, I was prepared for potential competitors coming to market. You can bet that no matter how far out you see the cultural swell that your product can ride on, you will not be the only one paddling to catch the wave. Yet for some reason I was still surprised to see it was happening so fast. Now I knew that there were a number of Americans running around with a similar idea. That meant we needed to move fast.

Driving away from the meeting, I felt encouraged and excited to work with Amacoco. For due diligence, however, we spent the next few days visiting a second producer. The experience couldn't have been more different. We were granted a meeting with one junior sales executive and he declined to let us tour their plant. We weren't allowed to meet the quality control manager, human resources, or visit the plantation and anyway, we were told, their supply came from a variety of farms. How did they ensure consistent quality? Oh, the quality was no problem, he said, it was always excellent.

Their lack of transparency and overconfidence didn't exactly leave me with a warm fuzzy feeling. The only potential good news was the price they quoted for production was cheaper than Amacoco. But they didn't pass the criteria we had established at the outset, particularly the transparency test, and we felt like we didn't know much more than before we visited. After meeting them face-to-face, I didn't want to do business with them.

Within a few weeks we had agreed that Amacoco would supply Zico for our New York launch. Juan Carlos would fly back to supervise the first production. If that went well we'd be ready to sign a long-term contract.

Early Investors: More Than Just a Check

So that took care of identifying our source of supply. We now had a chance, but no guarantee, that we'd have product for the Fancy Food

Show. And it was time to bring in more cash from investors. In April of 2004, with the Fancy Food Show just two months away, I gathered my early investors along with my team of consultants to El Salvador for a meeting. One of the investors was a senior executive at a large hotel group and had graciously volunteered a free meeting room at the Inter-Continental Hotel in San Salvador with a patio overlooking the pool.

I walked everyone through what we had learned, the plan of how we proposed to launch Zico, and then outlined the capital requirements, proposed business structure, and timing to go to market. My projection was that it would take us three years to be profitable, and we needed $1 million to launch and have eighteen to twenty-four months before we needed to raise more capital. I made it clear that if we were going to launch this year, we needed to walk out of this room with an agreement on two main things: the investment amount and term and my ownership and compensation.

The investors had lots of questions. Were we confident we could get what we needed, and what sort of supply contract could we sign with the producer? Who did we think would enter the market, and what would happen if an established beverage company decided to come out with their own coconut water? In answering all these questions, I didn't spin or try to reassure anyone. These were all the right questions to ask; all I could assure them was that I would dig into every one and address them as best as possible.

I then got into the details of how we would structure their investment. I proposed a $2 million pre-money (before the investment) valuation for Zico. I suggested to the nine early investors that they each contribute $100,000 in addition to the $20,000 that they already gave me as seed money. With that investment in Zico's coffers, the company would be worth about $3 million (called a post-money valuation) and we would have the $1 million I projected we needed to launch. For that $120,000 total investment they would each own 4 percent of the company. After I laid out my offer, there were a few moments of silence. A few people nodded their heads slightly as they considered, which I took as a good sign. But as people began to speak, I quickly realized I was in for an intense negotiation.

My friend Mike was one of the first to speak. He had been an investor in a few family businesses, and they always based ownership on capital contributed. "Mark, if the total investment in Zico would be a million dollars, shouldn't a $120,000 contribution purchase 12 percent of Zico? Maybe you would get something for your work to date, but 4 percent just sounds way too low." I was thinking, "What the hell, old buddy of mine? You're killing my deal!" But I realized if he's writing a check, then he's got the right to voice his opinion and decide like any other investor. (I also realized I should not have been negotiating with all of them at once, a mistake I would not make next time.) Other voices at the table chimed in with equally significant questions. Everyone agreed that the $2 million valuation was just too high for a company that was basically just one guy, some market research, and what was perhaps a good idea. Hernan added that my sales projections were optimistic: "I think you'll run out of money much sooner than you're projecting. I'm out."

Going into this meeting I knew that if I were an experienced entrepreneur raising money in Silicon Valley, no one would have blinked at a two-million-dollar valuation. But I wasn't a seasoned entrepreneur and this wasn't Silicon Valley, so I began to lay out other "walk away" scenarios that I had prepared.

I uncapped a dry-erase marker, cleaned the whiteboard, and started to write out some different options. Two hours later, we settled on a structure that we could all live with. We reduced the pre-money value of the company to $1 million, and therefore $1 million invested would own 50 percent of the company, and every investor who put in $120,000 would own 6 percent. Because I was selling significantly more of the company than I had planned, I got them to agree to a few concessions. The first was that I would draw a modest salary to increase when the business was cash flow positive. Though significantly less than I was making at the time, I knew it might be high given we had zero revenue; if only I had known that in the near future I wouldn't draw any salary at all for many months.

Second, I insisted that 50 percent of the investors' shares would be voting and 100 percent of mine would be. I might give up control on a true percentage ownership, but I wasn't ready to give it on a voting basis. Third, all involved agreed to contribute 1 percent of their equity stake to a social contribution fund or foundation, the objective of which I would determine at a later date.

Finally, I would have some additional upside in options or something that would allow me to earn more if they earned a good return on their investment.

Five from the group gave me a verbal commitment that day and the others seemed enthusiastic. In hindsight, I was offering an incredible deal. But, needless to say, no one gets to negotiate in hindsight. Like any long shot, the risk of losing it all was high, as was the pressure. I also realized that I probably could have held out, spent a few months finding other investors, and obtained a higher valuation. But with the cost of preparing for the Fancy Food Show already on the books, that wasn't an option and I was happy where I stood: I'd have investors whom I knew and trusted, and we'd be in the market within a few months.

The critical question was Hernan Bravo's: had I really raised enough money to launch a new brand properly? Now I can undoubtedly say no. As it turned out, Hernan's dire prediction would prove to be overly optimistic. I would end up burning through that first round of money in less than eight months after launch, forcing me to come back to this same group of investors three times over the next three years for additional capital.

Even if I had known at the time that I would need much more money to get Zico up and running, I'm not sure it would have mattered. The hallway outside that meeting room at the InterContinental wasn't filled with other investors banging on the door to get in on the deal. The truth was, I was raising as much money as I had access to, and I'd simply have to make do. Timing matters, and it's important to know where you are relative to the market for your type of company.

In reality, the early investment needs and structure of every start-up is unique. Sara Blakely started Spanx with $5,000 of her own money, never raised another dime from outside investors, and owns 100 percent of her billion-dollar brand. Doug Evans, founder of Juicero, raised $70 million before even launching his in-home fresh-pressed juice company. He said, "I wanted to have 60 months of cash and never have to ask for money again." And there are thousands of scenarios in-between. But no matter what, you can't avoid the fact that raising money is a royal pain in the you-know-what, both stressful and time consuming. But unless you're a trust-fund baby or the next Sara Blakely, here are a few suggestions based on both my successes and my mistakes, and on what I've seen other companies go through.

Be clear about what you need: Strive to estimate what you really need to execute your plan, or at least the first (or next) phase of growth and development. Generally speaking you should build an overly conservative cash flow model for twelve months. Whatever total capital you calculate you'll need, at least double it. It's always better to have a longer runway.

Control your destiny as long as possible: Try to sell no more than 30 percent of the company in any one round. This will keep you in control, protect your stake, and give you more to sell down the road if you need it. It's also hard to ensure your business will achieve your goals and maintain your values, especially in the first few years, if you're not captain of the ship. You will also determine what you ultimately own of the company based on what you sell in the early stages.

Choose your early partners carefully: All money may be green, but not all investors are the same. If you don't already personally know your early investors, spend time with them and vet them carefully before allowing them to invest. They should be aligned with your values and goals and be willing to support the mission of the company beyond just writing a check.

Raise what you can, when you can: Once you are clear on what you need, you feel like you have the right partners, are still in control, and can live with the terms of the deal, raise as much money as possible. Cash is king, and given the ups and downs of start-ups, it will inevitably run out sooner than expected so you want to have more cash in reserve. This is also a momentum game: once you have some investors interested, others will probably follow. There is no better time to raise money than when you don't need it.

IT WILL NOT BE THIS WAY

With the New York launch just a couple of months away, I thought things were going as well as could be expected on both the business and personal fronts. Each team member was coming through on their tasks, and it looked more and more likely that we would make it to the food show with actual product to hand out. Six of my early investors gave me a verbal commitment to contribute an additional $100,000 each, and Maura agreed we'd drain my 401(k) to invest as well.

The International Paper division I ran was also having a record year. Personally, I was a machine. I was incredibly productive, even more so since I was constantly prioritizing what was important. I ran or worked out regularly, ate well, meditated in the mornings, and believe it or not got a fair amount of sleep or at least filled in with naps. Even more critically, Maura and I seemed to be aligned, and she was intimately involved in every major decision about Zico and was committed to the vision and positive impact we hoped to make.

I thought I had achieved that elusive work-life synergy where every part of your life feeds the excitement of and engagement in every other part of your life. To some degree, I still think I had, but keeping so many balls up in the air is a tenuous thing. Small missteps can have major consequences.

I remember one night that busy spring when that became clear. I had arrived home one evening at the end of a weeklong, multi-country trip across South America, and Maura and I set aside the night to reconnect. For us this was a critical routine. During the two years we dated while in graduate school, our two years in Memphis, and the four years we lived in El Salvador, we had always found time and made it a priority to stay connected and to reconnect after time apart. The first day we were back together, we'd take a hike or go on a long walk or crack a bottle of wine and spend the evening listening to music, just us. We were amazed at how out of sync we could become after just a few days apart and at the same time how quickly we could reconnect, if we made the effort to do so. With two young girls, and my travel schedule, these moments became more difficult to arrange, and time after the kids went to sleep was golden.

That night, I had arrived home in time to help Maura feed and bathe our little girls and I read to them, played with them, scratched their backs, and sang them to sleep. Now the rest of the evening was ours. The music playing from our stereo echoed throughout the dining room and garden. I opened a bottle of wine and poured us each a glass. There was a cool breeze blowing through the dining room doors, and the view over San Salvador was spectacular. Maura's love of intimate, uninterrupted candlelit dinners, inherited from her parents, had converted me, and I usually relished this intentional disconnection from all the other stresses in our lives.

As a rule, I turned my phone off for every dinner but these days, with only a couple of months before the Fancy Food Show, I felt the need to be on call. With dinner fresh on the table, my phone rang and I saw it was my sister Mary Beth. Maura said not to answer but I reflexively hit the talk button instead and stepped away from the table. I knew Mary Beth was working feverishly to complete the packaging design, a critical item for us to meet our launch date. If it didn't get done, we ran the risk of missing the show, so for me there was no question; I had to take the call.

I was on with Mary Beth for no more than ten minutes. Sitting back down at the table, Maura was silent for a few moments, and then she put both hands on the table, sat up straight, and said slowly in a clear, strong, unequivocal voice, "It. Will. Not. Be. This. Way." She continued, "It will not be this way. It will NOT BE THIS WAY!" Her tone changed to one of deep concern and caring. "This is not what it's about, Mark. You've been away so much. You're always working. We've had so little time together. You hardly see the girls or me. We have got to draw some lines. What's the point if we have no life?"

My first reaction was to be absolutely pissed off. Didn't she understand how important this was? It was only a brief phone call. What would happen when things got really tough? Didn't she know I was doing this for us? For her? For the girls? Didn't she share the same dream? Had she forgotten how big this opportunity was? How much we had invested personally? The impact we could make on the world?

I thought of a million things I wanted to scream at her, but thank the heavens I bit my tongue. I was quiet and stared out to the city lights in the distance. I took a few deep breaths to calm myself and just listen: to her, to everything around me and inside of me. It all became clear. I looked across the table at the woman I loved, and said, "Okay. I get it. You're right. You're setting the bar higher. The question is: how do we make Zico a success and not lose what we have? How do we build a successful business while staying sane, together, connected, healthy, and happy? How do we make it work for us?"

That evening Maura drew her line in the sand and I decided how I wanted to live my life. We talked into the night about the damage starting a company might do to our personal lives, about supposedly successful businesspeople and entrepreneurs who had healthy bank accounts but toxic lives. The measure of Zico's success, we agreed, couldn't only be tallied at the end of the venture. You don't live life in retrospect, and we wanted to build a business that would be rewarding in real time. If we achieved that, if we were healthy, together, and truly happy, then we couldn't lose—even if the long-term financial rewards didn't materialize.

I knew of course there would be many late nights, weekend events, trips away. I knew it would be intense and stressful. But could I be present in the midst of that? Be aware and conscious of the choices I was making? If I chose to do something for work, then my goal would be to truly be there, not wishing I was and regretting I wasn't home. If I was home playing with my girls, then I would truly be there, not scheming the next big sale and worrying about inventory. We also knew there were risks. That this experience was going to test us in so many ways. But that night we reaffirmed our decision to go for it.

I also decided that night I would measure and manage life like I did my business: How many nights did I want to be home? Was I taking vacation time? Time with extended family? Meditating? Exercising? Reading? Taking time to just think? Those were equally important measures, and I would build them into a scorecard and track them just like sales and profit and loss.

This would be our goal. The intention we set. We'd soon have a chance to see how our ideal would play out in reality. Looking back this is one of the most critical moments in the history of Zico, in our relationship, and in our lives. It was a fulcrum point that led to where we are today. The truth is that there would be many other "it will not be this way" moments, and each time we'd have to find a way to get back on the same page. But we kept coming back to our intention to achieve success as we defined it, to recommit to reaching higher.

THE POWER OF HABITS

When young entrepreneurs ask me about the early days of Zico, soon after the questions of where the idea came from, how we launched, and how we came up with the name come the ones about work-life balance. They want to know if and how I managed to stay healthy, sane, married, and be a good parent, especially through the crunch times. They want tips and solutions. I tell them there's no magic formula and there are also no rights and wrongs, just decisions and consequences— but healthy habits certainly help.

That night after Maura declared that it will not be this way, I knew I needed to operate differently or I'd never get everything done at work and home. I didn't want to be an absentee husband or father with a two-year-old and a newborn. Looking back, I realize a few things I did right at this stage that allowed me to get through this time, accomplish what I needed to do, and that helped me survive and even thrive during the insanity that would be our Zico journey and is the case for most start-ups.

PLAN, PRIORITIZE, EXECUTE, REPEAT

Early in my career, I used to have the bad habit of putting off my most important tasks until the end of the day. My logic was to clear the decks in order to give my most challenging projects my full attention. So I'd begin my day by writing my to-do list and then start working through my e-mail queue, which would lead to phone calls and inevitable meetings. The problem, as you might guess, is that the deck never seemed to get clear. I'd try to get to the key tasks at the end of the day, but I was inevitably tired, not clearheaded, and anxious to get home and see Maura.

I finally started to take to heart the advice of Stephen Covey to do first things first. I would start my day by deciding what were the most important two to three objectives for the week: What tasks, if I accomplished them, would move the needle, and would I celebrate that night? At the end of the week? At the end of the month or year?

This way of thinking about my goals necessitated me being clear about what I wanted to accomplish. What was really important? What would move the business forward? What was aligned with my boss's goals? Maybe it was one or two big deals that were in the works, or a major new marketing initiative or sales tracking system. Once I was clear on those (and my boss agreed), I'd work on the top priorities every morning for a few hours without looking at e-mail or even answering the phone. I felt an immediate sense of purpose and accomplishment that energized me for the rest of the day. I could be more present and aware in meetings or on calls or plowing through e-mail knowing I had already accomplished something important. I got home at a more reasonable hour. I began to see results, and my boss and co-workers took notice. I began to take fifteen to twenty minutes in the evening and on Sunday to look at my list of objectives for the year, month, and week, and reorganize or reprioritize what was most important.

I started to apply this process more generally to my life: What did I want to accomplish personally? Learn other languages? Travel to countries? Write a book? Make a positive social impact? Achieve financial security? I started to apply this planning and commitment to first things first to everything. Friends and family would laugh that I was a planning junkie, especially since they had never known me to be the most organized guy. This was the new me.

By the time we were gearing up for Zico, my daily routine was prioritized by putting the most important things first, so I dove in even further, getting very clear written goals and priorities, and began to add techniques I learned from reading Jack Canfield (i.e., identifying limiting beliefs), Tony Robbins (all you ever need is inside you now), and other personal productivity experts.

Remarkably, you can survive, even prosper, in a corporate environment with incredibly poor work habits. The organization has its own momentum, and if you're good in a meeting and responsive to the day-to-day requests for your attention, you can cruise along for quite a while. It's amazing how you can fill ten-, twelve-, or fifteen-hour days doing very little that is really important, and in fact do so for years or for an entire career. With the momentum of your start-up completely on your shoulders, however, this sort of work style spells certain death, which was a lesson it would take me a while to learn.

TIME TO MAKE THE LEAP

Two hours after our plane landed at Kennedy Airport, we walked into the cavernous Javits Center. The place was a beehive of activity with thousands of workers and entrepreneurs from around the world bus-ily setting up their booths. I was again struck by the fear that our ef-fort would get lost in the noise of all this activity. Using the published map of the conference room floor, I saw Zico was in booth number 5250. We went to that booth location. There was a booth set up—but it wasn't Zico. The guide was wrong! Our location was two aisles over. I grew even more worried.

When I finally located the Zico booth and took a look, I thought, "Thank you, Sister!" I had seen pictures of all the pieces, but all put together it was a visual and functional masterpiece. Among all the crude booths and cheesy Kinko's-produced banners, Mary Beth had created a visual and physical oasis. The ten-by-twenty-foot space had a mythical, tropical sky-blue background that was exactly like the Zico packaging and a white floor with a large oval table at the center with three round recessed coolers, one for each flavor: natural, mango, and passion fruit. Bar stools surrounded the table, and there were ex-pansive benches framing the booth, which doubled as storage bins and were topped with inflatable cushions in Zico blue.

The show opened to the public at nine a.m. the following morning and we were there at eight a.m. to make sure everything was set. Mary Beth was making last-minute tweaks to make the booth perfect. Maura was getting the badge scanner set up and organizing pamphlets. Ro-berto and Jose were loading coolers with product and had roped their wives into helping. Mercedes was putting out sampling cups. Jon Os-mundsen had press releases to take to the media room, where reporters and others from the press would gather. Everyone looked great: the guys in matching white, Cuban, athletic-cut Guayabera shirts, women in light blue Zico tees and white pants.

I gathered everyone around and went over the plan. Watch peo-ple's badges, I reminded them. Red was for retailers and yellow for press. Green are other exhibitors so less important, but everyone should be treated as a potential consumer. Remember the key messages and stay focused, no distractions in the booth area like food or cell phones. Take a break when you need to but make sure two or more people in the booth know where you're going. Scan badges of people who want more information, and if you take business cards, write a little note so we can remember who someone is and what they were interested in. If the Zico is not cold, don't sample it but even then remember, there *will* be some people that hate this stuff! If they look like they're going to gag, take them by the arm and politely escort them to the side and remind them it's an acquired taste for some people. Get them away. No spitting out the product inside the booth!

By eleven a.m. we had people three deep and we were handing out samples at a rate that made me worry we wouldn't have enough to last. I wasn't sure that the people in the back of the crowd knew what we were giving out; was it food, beverage, or new hand cream? But once the booth had created a certain amount of social gravity, the crowd's excitement seemed to feed off itself.

The interest was so intense it was a task just to scan badges or take business cards and keep track of who we were talking to. The people coming to the booth were from every conceivable side of the global consumer goods business—store owners, distributors, buyers for chains large and small. There were writers, reporters, and college students learning about the industry. There were marketers, ingredient producers, consultants, and lawyers.

I got in so many conversations that, at times, I wasn't sure if I was selling or being sold. Many of these first conversations were a little embarrassing. Much of the lingo of the business was new to me, and I had to walk the line between using these encounters to become better informed and not looking like a complete idiot. Questions that I either didn't understand or couldn't answer were coming my way every other minute. Often, the best I could do was take their business card, scan their badge, and promise that I'd get back to them with an answer soon.

Worse yet, I often didn't realize exactly who I was talking to and therefore how high the stakes of the conversation were. At one point Roberto introduced me to "Brian from Fairway." Breezily, I started to tell him all about how coconut water was the best way to rehydrate after workouts, completely missing that this was *the* Fairway where I had wandered the aisles and a critical New York account. Meanwhile he just wanted to order a pallet load of Zico.

After two days of working the show, Maura and I retreated to our hotel room, physically and mentally drained. It was impossible to know exactly what that constant whirlwind of activity had added up to. As we were relaxing and getting ready for a celebratory dinner with our team, we had CNBC on in the room. Suddenly, the host introduced a news segment about the convention. I recognized the long wavy gray hair and mustache of the reporter. He was at our booth asking lots of questions, but I didn't have a clue who he was.

"So, Phil," the host intoned, "anything interesting at the Fancy Food Show this year?" When the camera turned to Phil Lempert, the so-called Supermarket Guru, he was sitting at a desk with a number of products in front of him. My eyes went straight to the little blue Tetra Pak that clearly said Zico. Phil started in by talking about a new salsa and a tasty new cracker line. Then he held up a package of Zico and said, "And then there's coconut water. Known as a natural source of electrolytes, replenishment, and nutrition across the tropical world. I think coconut water is going to be the next big thing. Watch for it." The host was back on camera and, with an expression that suggested he was far from convinced, said, "Ah, yeah, I was just thinking that I needed some coconut water." He chuckled. "I guess we'll just have to wait and see on that one, Phil."

For the two-minute segment I sat on the edge of the bed with my mouth open. Maura had the wherewithal to grab her cell phone and snap a picture of the screen. After it was over, Maura put a hand on my shoulder. "Well, if we needed a sign, that was it," she said.

She continued, "Time to go all in. How long until you can quit IP?"

We had booked out the back room of a cool, funky restaurant and bar in the Meatpacking District called Son Cubano to celebrate with the team. We ate, danced salsa and merengue, and drank enough Zico-ritas to fill a bathtub until the wee hours of the morning. We were about to embark on a wild ride and we knew it.

CHAPTER 6

GIVE UNTIL IT HURTS

Not long after the New York show, I flew to Memphis in July 2004 to meet my boss and resign from my IP job in person. When I told him I was resigning to start my own business, he was taken aback. "But I have just been working on your potential next move," he said. "Can I at least tell you about it?" He told me he had a plum new assignment for me: head of International Paper's global tobacco packaging business. IP sold the rolls of paper that went to make cigarette packaging and carton boxes to everyone from Philip Morris to local producers in Indonesia. It was a billion-dollar global business.

This was a big promotion and considered one of the key roles along the way to becoming a senior executive. Do a great job for a few years and I'd have all sorts of opportunities. One of my career goals was to run a billion-dollar global business. But certainly not this one. I smiled and thanked him profusely for considering me but, I told him, my mind was made up. Had I been wavering in my decision in the slightest, the prospect of taking that job would have sealed it. A high-paying corporate job running packaging for tobacco was my personal nightmare—a true selling-my-soul scenario.

FIND YOUR BEACHHEAD

Now that I would soon be freed from my corporate job (along with its reliable paycheck), Maura and I started to debate where we should move to in order to launch Zico. Major corporations often choose smallish markets, such as Columbus, Ohio, or Indianapolis, Indiana, to soft-launch their new products and test consumer reactions to refine their strategy before launching nationally. We didn't have the money for a soft launch and the idea didn't appeal to me anyway. I wanted a big market that had dozens of diverse consumer groups so we could experiment with multiple tactics and figure out who our core consumers and retailers would be. I'd likely only have one shot at this, so there was no point in succeeding in a market with limited growth potential.

We also wanted to launch somewhere we wanted to live. We needed to find something that was right for the business but also fit into our life plans. Three cities met the criteria: New York, Los Angeles, and Miami. Though Maura greatly preferred L.A. or Miami strictly based on warmer weather, I argued that we should spend a few years in New York first and then move to one of the other cities. Although she didn't like the cold or the bustle of New York, where she had grown up, it had the advantage of being close to her family so our daughters would log some quality grandparent time.

New York also offered a hugely diverse group of potential consumers and had the added advantage of being the media capital of the U.S., and arguably the world, so if we were successful it would hopefully echo everywhere. Jose and Roberto were based in New Jersey, just outside of New York, and they offered to lease us some of their office space. We'd have one office, share a conference room and a receptionist.

Next we dove into the tricky New York metro real estate market. Maura wanted a house, not an apartment, so Manhattan was out of the running. She had grown up in Westchester County but the prices there were too high for us, so we decided to focus on northern New Jersey. We found a house we liked and could afford in a lovely little town called Oradell and made an offer on it, all while visiting family in Rhode Island. I'll admit I did some creative storytelling about our finances to get the loan. Fortunately, this was 2004, pre–mortgage crisis, and no one seemed to be very concerned about what people put on those financial forms at the time. We had put every free dollar we had into Zico, so we had to take a loan from both Maura's and my parents to come up with the down payment but again, it felt like with home prices skyrocketing and Zico about to become huge, we'd pay them back in no time.

Good news was swirling around Zico the summer of 2004 after the Fancy Food Show. The brand was featured in the *New York Sun*, the *Journal News*, *Food & Wine*, *Jane* magazine, *Better Homes and Gardens*, and dozens of health and wellness blogs and websites. The Cascadia branding and marketing group voted Zico the hottest new beverage of 2004. I was sure this was the sort of momentum that would just keep building.

While I was winding down my work at IP, I asked Jose and Roberto to hire a small team of two to three salespeople, open bank accounts, rent a van, conduct some demos and marketing on the side, and start generating some sales. I'd complete my move from El Salvador by late October and jump into the day-to-day. I thought we'd receive our first full container load of product by July and have it on shelves around New York by August. I hoped we'd be able to do $400,000 in sales by the end of the year, generating enough margin to cover most of our expenses. In early 2005, we would have made enough of a splash to make a deal with a major distributor, and then we would be off to the races. I figured from there we could do $2 million in sales for 2005. In five years, I planned to be in six major cities with—and let's just pick a nice round number—$10 million in annual sales. From there, we'd introduce other coconut-related products, expand nationwide, then go global, and finally take over the universe. It all seemed so achievable.

SLOW OUT OF THE GATE

But no, it wasn't meant to be that easy. The main problem was that our sales projections for the first couple of months were proving to have no relationship with reality. On the positive side, we did start out with some remarkably prestigious accounts. The Beverly Hills Four Seasons bought twenty cases and paid for them to be shipped to Los Angeles, as did Las Ventanas, a super-high-end resort in Los Cabos, Mexico. By the end of September 2004, we had about eighty accounts across New York City, including multiple locations for Better Burger, Health Nuts, Garden of Eden, and the Amish Market. We had a few small natural foods stores, cafes and delis, the two new Equinox gyms, and six Bikram yoga studios. Fairway, the account I had nearly fumbled at the Fancy Food Show when I met Brian, the buyer, was our biggest account ordering regularly, sometimes fifty or one hundred cases at a time.

Although I had confidence in our product regardless, these first sales were psychologically huge. I would see every order that came through and share it with Maura immediately. Who cares if it was only five cases for a Bikram yoga studio on the Upper West Side, and billed out less than seventy-five dollars? It was another order! With this first set of customers, Roberto, Jose, and I were not only just trying to move cases but also to discern patterns. Who was buying and why? With what frequency?

As exciting and interesting as all this was, the problem was that there just weren't nearly enough sales coming in. Given that we were self-distributing to learn the market, it took more time than we had expected to find the right accounts, call on them, get them to buy, and return with a delivery. Zico's monthly burn rate was exacerbated by line items I hadn't even considered putting in the financial model. Parking tickets for instance, which for some months were more expensive than the lease on our delivery van. One depressing week, the cost of the parking tickets even outpaced our sales revenue. Also, slow sales meant carrying more inventory than expected. Our warehouse costs were killing us.

Even if we were lucky enough to get Zico into an account, we had to follow up to see if it sold or not. The Bikram studio owners or managers would call when they were low but not the Korean deli owner down the street. They expected us to magically appear at just the point they were out of stock.

Chain stores posed their own set of problems and arcane and seemingly endless lists of rules and restrictions. It often took weeks just to get a meeting. When we finally met with the Whole Foods buyer for the northeast region, we learned we had just missed the beginning of a quarterly purchasing process but could probably make the next one in three months. We ran into similar issues with other chains like Gristedes, Food Emporium, Associated, and Duane Reade with the added complication of being asked to pay upward of $50,000 in so-called slotting fees if we wanted to get on the shelf. The way these stores had set up their supply chains certainly wasn't built for the little guy to break in easily.

Of course, if we didn't show up at just the right time, we left an opening all too easy for our new competitor Vita Coco to exploit. I had begun to see Vita Coco showing up in more and more accounts.

As the weather started to turn in late September, I knew we were in trouble. We were selling less than $10,000 each month when I expected to be closer to $100,000. We just weren't going to get there fast enough, and now we were facing the winter months when, I had learned, beverage sales fall by 30 percent or more.

GIVE UNTIL IT HURTS

Though we had interest from major distributors like United Natural Foods (UNFI), KeHE, and local beverage distributors in New Jersey, Texas, and Massachusetts as well as importers in the UK, Japan, Korea, and Barbados, I remained committed to the idea that we had to prove our concept in New York before we expanded. Roberto had identified the leading distributors in New York, and we had conversations with Steiner Foods, Boylan, Dora's Naturals, Island Natural, and a group of Korean distributors. While we were evaluating all these options, one distributor's name kept coming up: Big Geyser.

Big Geyser was the beverage kingmaker in New York City and, arguably, the country. They were (and still are) the dominant player for independent (basically non-Coke or -Pepsi), nonalcoholic beverage distribution in New York and one of the most important and influential distributors in the industry. The company had a network of over one hundred route owners who served in excess of twenty thousand accounts. They delivered beverages to the big chains as well as convenience stores, gas stations, restaurants, hotels, colleges, hospitals, corporate cafeterias, drugstores, ethnic markets, delis, bodegas, and natural food stores. Big Geyser had been credited with being integral to the success of the hottest upstart brands in the industry including: Vitaminwater, Smartwater, Nantucket Nectars, Fuze, Mistic, and Apple & Eve.

Geyser also had a reputation for being tough and demanding. While they had made some brands a mega-success, many brand owners feared that dealing with Big Geyser only had two outcomes: either you became a huge success or you died on the vine under their exclusivity clause, never able to get their attention while contractually restricted from putting your product on New York shelves in any other way. I figured we would sign one of the other distributors first, build the business, gain strength and resources, and then go to Big Geyser when we were ready to scale.

By late 2004, we knew we were getting some attention from Big Geyser, at least at the street level. Two Bikram studio owners in Manhattan told me their Big Geyser sales rep was pissed that they weren't reordering as much Vitaminwater as usual. "What is all this Zico crap stacked in the hallway and who the hell is selling it to you?" he wanted to know.

In October, I was talking with a beverage industry person about our distribution quandary when she said she knew Irving "Hal" Hershkowitz, the owner of Big Geyser, well enough to make an introduction. Did I want to meet him? I said I wasn't sure and that it seemed too early. "Take the meeting," she urged. "What can it hurt?"

Big H, as he was known, was a legend in the beverage industry. He was supposedly the highest-volume liquor salesman in the world in the early 1980s working for a local distributor. In the mid-eighties he saw bottled water becoming popular in high-end New York restaurants and decided to start distributing them and other natural beverages and juices, believing they were the future. His insight and timing were perfect. He was also brilliant about the way he organized his business. Rather than have all the cost and hassle of employing hundreds of drivers and salespeople, he "sold" the rights to individuals and small operators to distribute his brands in a given territory. These independent distributors bought from Big Geyser and resold to the retailers in their territory that might only be a forty-square-block area of Manhattan. Hal was supposed to be shrewd and tough as nails, but his drivers, who could make solid six figures working their areas, were the real hard-core street operators.

I met Hershkowitz in a nice Upper East Side diner. He was a big man who radiated power and confidence. He didn't stand up and, except for shaking my hand, kept eating his breakfast as I sat down and put a carton of Zico on the table. "So tell me about it," he said with a mouthful of eggs. I went into my sales pitch: the benefits of coconut water, the potential market, and our expansion plans.

When I hit the end of my sales pitch he looked at me and thought for a moment. "I like it," he said in a heavy New York accent. "My guys need something ethnic. I hear you're making some noise in some yoga studios, too. Good to cross over. Few brands can do that. We'll take it in and roll it out in the spring. One thing you gotta know, though. This is a tough business. You gotta be ready to give until it hurts and then give some more. Once everyone makes money on it, then maybe you'll make some money."

I have to admit it was a heart-pounding moment: a cross between getting drafted into the big leagues and getting sentenced to jail time.

"One more thing," he said, "only thing I don't like about it is that you got no patent or trademark on coconut water. In five years there might be a dozen brands selling basically the same thing. You better move fast if you want to still be around." *Five years?* I thought. *I'll be lucky to be around in five months.*

THEIR WAY OR THE HIGHWAY

As Big H had instructed, I shipped his son Lewis some cases of Zico, a presentation overview, and samples of all our promotional material, and showed up for a meeting with him and some other Big Geyser executives the following week. No sooner had I sat down in their clean, modern, but not too ostentatious conference room than Lewis launched into me.

"Look. We got your samples and presentation," he said without preamble. "We've talked to some people about it and I gotta tell ya, I don't like it. I don't get it. It tastes like dirty socks and I don't know who's gonna buy it. But you're in luck. My father and my brother like it. I'm still known around here as the guy who hated Vitaminwater. Apparently, if I think it's crap it's going to do great. Plus my father says we're taking it in, so we'll take it in.

"Harold will send you the contract," he said. "When you are ready to sign, tell him. But let me tell you one thing: People will tell you that we build brands. We don't build brands. At least not at the beginning. You do. You do the work. Get my guys excited. Build some momentum, and then we'll take it from there. But you gotta be ready to do the dirty work for as long as it takes."

The next day I received the contract via e-mail from Harold. When I started through it I could hardly believe what I was reading. Every section, every term, every condition benefited them. They had multiple ways to arbitrarily drop Zico, for instance, while my only exit was after three years to buy them out by paying them the equivalent of their gross profit for the previous eighteen months. I had seen and signed a fair number of contracts in my career, and had never seen anything like this.

I switched to "track changes" mode in Word and started to go to town with changes that I thought were reasonable. I then sent it to my lawyer, who inserted a couple dozen more. A few days later I sent it back to Harold with a nice note saying we were excited to work together as long as we could work through some of the contract issues. I got a call within an hour from Harold. "Mark, I got your e-mail and I don't think you understand. The contract I sent you is the contract. Period. There will be no changes. That's it."

I tried to explain my concerns but he wouldn't budge. It was literally their way or the highway, as in: me getting on the highway to continue to deliver my own product.

Still optimistic that there was at least some room to negotiate, I whittled down the changes to just a few I thought were critical and a few days later sent it again. Another call from Harold followed: "Look, Mark, you can do this a hundred times and the answer is the same. The contract is the contract. Brands much larger than yours have signed the exact same contract." He added, "And by the way, I assume you know Vita Coco? Nice guys. Little aggressive but that's not such a bad thing. They've been hounding us to carry their brand and make a pretty good case and say they're willing to accept any conditions we give them." I asked if we could arrange a meeting with him and Lewis again. "Sure," he said, "but let's not waste too much time here."

Roberto and I met with Lewis and Harold a few days later. It was pretty clear that Big Geyser thought they had us in a corner. To drive the point home, on a side table sat a case of Vita Coco right next to a case of Zico. The message was obvious: they had options and we did not. "Coconut water is coconut water, right?" Lewis said as he pulled out samples of Zico and Vita Coco from their cases. "I like your packaging better but what's the real difference?"

While I talked through the differences—the brand, our strategy, taste profile—Roberto picked up the case of Vita Coco and inspected it and took one package out. He then took two glasses set out on the conference table and poured Zico into one and Vita Coco into the other. The Zico was clear and translucent. The Vita Coco came out with a slight brownish hue.

"Which one do you want to drink?" Roberto said simply.

"Okay, that's disgusting," Lewis said, examining the Vita Coco. "Who would drink that?" I jumped in to explain that coconut water was very sensitive and there were many challenges to getting it right.

How we had carefully selected our Brazilian supplier for their ability to produce a consistent, light, clean product and taste. Our supplier wasn't perfect but they were the best out there today. How Vita Coco was using another producer that we had eliminated because our research with the University of Florida beverage center discovered problems with consistency and quality control. "Looks like Vita might be running into those, um, challenges," I added.

With the two glasses on the table giving me some leverage, I changed the topic. "Look, I understand your position on the contract. I'm ready to sign," I told him. "I only want one concession. I want Zico to be your exclusive coconut water. That would allow us to know you're committed and help us justify putting most of our marketing and brand-building efforts in New York."

"I figured you'd ask for that," Lewis said. "We've talked about it. No problem. But you better be ready for a fight. Those Vita guys are aggressive and in this business, aggressive is good."

Once out of their office building, I stopped Roberto in the parking lot. "How the hell did you know that that package of Vita Coco was a bad one?" I asked. He explained that a manager at a bodega on the Upper West Side had recently pulled some Vita off his shelves because a customer complained. "He showed it to me and I remembered the expiration date," he said. "It was the same on the packages they had on the table, so I figured there was a good chance."

"Bold," I said. "Fucking bold."

One bright spot that fall was Fairway Market. Fairway's Upper West Side location was a New York institution since the 1950s. I'm sure the fact that Zico was in their stores and doing well was one of the reasons we'd caught the attention of Big Geyser. I made an at-least-twice-weekly pilgrimage to their Upper West Side store to personally check in and chat up the store manager Jose, who had given us a display at the head of an aisle (a coveted spot called an "endcap display" in the business). Walking into the store in early December, just as I was negotiating with Big Geyser, I was distressed to find that our endcap display had been replaced with mulled wine and kosher apple sauce. The beginning of Hanukkah had bumped Zico to the back of the store, and I knew that was going to kill our sales. Jose was apologetic but had more bad news. After the Hanukkah products the space would be reserved for sparkling cider for Christmas and then panettone for New Year's. "You can probably get the display back in late January," he told me, "definitely by March." It was going to be a long, lean winter.

All of this might have been tolerable if the general level of unhappiness around our house was not so high. Though from New York originally, Maura had left years ago and was miserable in the cold weather and missed El Salvador. With the move, the new business, and renovating our new house with toddlers in tow, we were all exhausted and overwhelmed. Before Thanksgiving, our daughter Lexi was hit with a stomach flu so severe that we had to check her into a hospital to get her rehydrated with an IV. Nothing would stay down—not even Zico, which had always worked. Not long after that, the basement of our house flooded in a storm. Perhaps inviting Maura's family to Christmas would put us all in a better mood, we thought. On Christmas Eve with a full house of guests, the sewer backed up. If Maura and I had been in a better place, we might have been able to laugh about a run of bad luck. No one was laughing.

We went to stay with Maura's parents in Rhode Island to celebrate the New Year. We toasted the departure of 2004, happy to see it in the rearview mirror but also trying to honor all the effort we had put into it. We were sure 2005 was going to be the payoff for all that hard work.

I dropped by the office the following day, even though it was technically a holiday, and started sorting through a pile of mail. At the bottom of the pile I opened an envelope addressed to "President, Zico LLC." I assumed it was junk mail until I noticed the return address: New Jersey Office of the U.S. Department of Agriculture. My mind went quickly to the four shipping containers of Zico that were somewhere in transit from Brazil. My heart sank when I opened the letter: "NOTICE OF EMBARGO" it read in big block letters. Not a great way to kick off 2005.

STRAITJACKET

Late in January 2005 the temperature had risen only slightly above freezing when I left for my run at five a.m. Snow fluttered through the air when I started out but it was drizzling a freezing rain by the time I returned. It was a Saturday so there was no need to get the girls up and off to school, and Maura was still in bed upstairs. I was having flashes of thinking that maybe I didn't want to be an entrepreneur or take a swing at the big time anymore. But we were in far too deep to change course. It would be like the captain jumping out of a small but sinking ship before the crew.

I sat down at my computer and opened Skype to prepare for the conference call I had scheduled with Geoff Abbott, who would be logging on from Australia. I had met Geoff in El Salvador as he was completing his research on cross-cultural integration by managers for his PhD in coaching. I paid him as a coach when I started Zico. When I told him I could no longer pay for his services, he told me not to worry about the bill for a while, that he wanted to see me through the tough times.

My Skype phone rang. In his regularly cheery Australian accent, Geoff said, "So how's it going, Mark?"

"Honestly," I said, "not well, Geoff. Not well at all."

I went on a little monologue describing my tragic situation, that sales were slow, that I had cut everything I could think of, and how we were running through our last cash reserves. If that weren't enough, the USDA had put four containers of Zico under quarantine. We weren't going to make it through the quarter and we'd probably lose the house. Maura was depressed. The girls were sick. And we all missed El Salvador.

I couldn't help thinking how the optimism had vanished and both Maura and I felt so uncertain about what lay ahead. Maura would often ask, "Can I just push the fast-forward button to get through this part and see how things pan out?" I tried to reassure her but underneath I was worried as well. Even if Zico succeeded, I realized, we might remain deeply conflicted about whether it was worth the price we were paying. If Maura's feelings weren't unnerving enough, I overheard our daughter Ciara explain to a friend: "We were really happy in El Salvador and then my dad had to move us to New Jersey to start Zico."

When I finally ran out of terrible news, Geoff let a moment of silence go by.

"Mark, I'm so sorry to hear all this but is it really all that bad?" he said. His response was more than a little aggravating. Yes, I told him, things were that bad. Losing my home, all of our money and that of our investors, the specter of declaring bankruptcy. How much worse could it be?

"Okay," he said, "I want you to go to your front window and look outside."

"What are you talking about, Geoff?"

"Just humor me," he said. So I picked up the laptop and walked to the front window of the house.

"What do you see?" he asked. I told him I just saw trees and the lawn and the street.

"Do you see a white van?" No, I said. "Okay, good. And there are no guys outside in white jumpsuits in your driveway?" No. "So you're telling me there are not two guys that are going to put you in a strait-jacket, throw you in the back of a van, and put you in a padded room for the next twenty years?" I said no.

"Then what the hell are you complaining about, Mark?"

"Okay, I see your point," I said.

"I'm not sure you do, Mark," he said. "Let me try to be clear. You are still young, you have a beautiful family. You're happily married. You're well educated. Zico might do great or it might collapse; either way you and your family have about a zero percent chance of going hungry. I think you'll probably figure some way out of this but if you don't, you'll find another opportunity. You cannot control everything that is coming at you but you can control how you react."

Later that morning I sat alone thinking about what Geoff had said. I had been looking for sympathy and he served up some tough love. The truth was that I wasn't used to facing major setbacks in my life. The other social structures that I had been a part of—college, the Peace Corps, graduate school, and as an employee at major corporations—were much more forgiving than the make-or-break re-alities of the start-up world. Before, there had always been a support system, a boss or a teacher or a team member, to pitch in or give guid-ance. If I failed at a project, I usually got a second and sometimes a third chance. I was new to facing the potential of real failure, and because of that I took every downturn like a bullet.

It would take a while for Geoff's sage advice to sink in, a good year at least, but I had begun to realize a fundamental truth. What Geoff helped me remember was that no matter how bad things got, by any reasonable measure (and certainly relative to the billions in the world who are in true poverty and desperation) I was incredibly fortunate. Yes, things hadn't gone exactly as planned since the launch seven months ago at the Fancy Food Show. In fact, nothing had gone according to plan. But the truth was, Zico—while running deep in the red—was still running.

Our financial situation was no doubt very serious. But it wasn't life threatening nor was it a true existential threat to who I was. Like Geoff had reminded me, I wouldn't be any less of a loving father if I failed. Nor would I be any less of a husband, son, brother, or human for that matter, especially if I tended to those sides of me along the way.

But what if this failure lasted a lifetime? What if I never fully recovered financially or in my career? What then?

To try to sort out what was truly important, a friend suggested I try what is called the Eulogy Exercise.

How would I want people to speak about me at my eulogy? I basically came up with two scenarios. In the first, I am recognized as a brilliant entrepreneur who amassed a huge fortune. University buildings and art museums have been named after me, and I helped make a major impact in the beverage and other industries. Looking down from on high, I see only two of three ex-wives are at my funeral and I know they are fighting tooth and nail with my young fourth bride over my estate. All my kids are there, but I hardly recognize them because I haven't seen them in years and in fact was rarely part of their lives. I see a few friends but the crowd is mainly business associates, some of whom talk about how I screwed them over on the path to success.

In the second scenario, my funeral is a small celebration-of-life ceremony held at my favorite beach with thirty or so close friends and family. Maura (my one and only wife), my two beautiful daughters, their young families, my siblings, and my closest friends are all there. I made a decent living but never had a lot of money. I contributed to my local community but never made a big impact on the world. But I was a good man. I was there for my kids and grandkids and other friends and even strangers in need. Some of the attendees recall that

I had once taken a shot on a crazy business idea called Zico. It flopped but I had moved on with my life. Other entrepreneurs had picked up the mantle and built coconut water into a major global business that made a positive impact on the world. I never envied them their success. The success I had achieved had been far more personal.

Obviously these were extreme scenarios, and of course I'd ideally like to have the best elements of both. But the exercise reminded me that no amount of money or status in business could make that first scenario appealing. And the remarkable truth was that I had most of the second scenario already in my life. I was already winning in ways I deemed most meaningful.

After putting my fear and ego in proper perspective, I began to see that the problems I was facing with Zico were only insurmountable if they stopped me from moving forward. The USDA embargo was a perfect example. I started to think about each problem, one at a time, and figure out how to solve it and move on. I got clear on what the FDA's concerns were and I found a lawyer with experience in these sorts of disputes as well as a renowned food scientist. I assembled the necessary data, completed the forms, created the reports, scheduled the meetings. I broke down the problem into manageable steps and plowed forward.

In the end, I was able to avoid a product recall and prove that it was just a paperwork filing issue. I voluntarily re-exported $50,000 worth of product that had not been put on shelves, which we donated to the relief effort for the victims of the South Asian tsunami that had just occurred. With the correct filings in place we were able to start a new production run that would arrive in time for the Big Geyser launch.

On the financing front, I had met with numerous potential investors since we launched, but in the end the same existing investors committed an additional $500,000 in early 2005, eight months after they wrote their first checks. Though not the $5 million I hoped to raise, it was enough to keep us solvent through the year.

I took a similar yeoman-like attitude toward my mental health. On my morning runs, I would count my blessings and then repeat mantras out loud to myself. "All I ever need is inside me now," and "I am thankful for my body, which is healthy and strong; for my mind, which is sharp and clear; and for my spirit, which can't be beat." I'm sure my neighbors might have thought I was unhinged chanting this as I left for my four-thirty-a.m. runs, and I don't have scientific studies to prove that this sort of positive psychology has much effect, but I can tell you that it helped me to stay focused on the tasks at hand and keep perspective at the same time.

THE MEAN STREETS

In March of 2005, nine months after introducing Zico to the world, I had my shot at the big leagues when I was given a chance to address the hundred or so route owners of Big Geyser in advance of our spring launch with them. These were the men (and they were all men) who would be delivering (and hopefully selling) Zico into new accounts. The route owners all started their day at a Big Geyser central warehouse in Maspeth, Queens, and from there fanned out in delivery trucks to every corner of the five boroughs of New York City and Long Island, covering almost two thousand square miles, twenty thousand accounts, and a population of fifteen million.

These route owners were basically running their own businesses under the umbrella of Big Geyser, and their buy-in was critical to the success of any brand they carried. They were hardworking street guys from various walks of life, but what they had in common was none of them were pushovers. They worked in a cutthroat cash business and the daily grind of fighting New York traffic, negotiating with penny-pinching store owners, battling other distributors for precious shelf space, and often butting heads with Big Geyser themselves, put them in perpetually bad moods. They were allergic to sales pitches, fluff marketing, and bullshit in any form.

Maura and I arrived at six a.m., thirty minutes before the meeting was scheduled to start, and found parking down the street from Geyser's warehouse, in front of what looked like a garbage processing depot. It was still pitch-black, freezing cold, and the pothole-lined sidewalk was a mix of slush, gravel, and ice. We entered the open-air, unheated warehouse filled with delivery trucks.

In the time since the rollout at the food show, we had hired a small team and had a few college students working part-time doing demos and events. I had all of them come to this presentation in the hopes of looking like a bigger organization than we were. In truth, only three (counting me) of the eight were full-time employees.

We met a few people on the warehouse floor and followed the crowd as it moved down a small hallway. Most of the people who I took to be the route owners and Big Geyser salespeople flowed into a separate room. The rest of us, all taking off heavy coats and hats to display branded shirts—Vitaminwater, Fuze, Mistic, GuS Soda—muddled around outside noshing on bagels, donuts, sausage, and eggs, which I assumed was the breakfast Zico had sponsored for $1,000. As the new brand on the block, we were told that buying the breakfast was our "opportunity" to do something nice for the Big Geyser route owners.

Every ten or fifteen minutes, for the next hour, a little man would open the meeting room door, poke his head out, and call the next brand on the agenda: "Fuze!" or "Mistic!" then "Vitaminwater!" One team would funnel out and the other march into the room. The Vitaminwater team must have been twenty strong and looked like a college frat party, bros and cute sorority girls included. Their energy carried into the room and when the door closed we heard laughter and banter flying back and forth. Then it was calm for a few minutes. Then dead silence and some yelling, followed by a huge uproar. The door flew open and out stormed a couple of route owners clearly in a huff. The Vitaminwater guys came out a few minutes later, yucking it up.

"How did it go?" I asked the young guy who appeared to be the head of the Vitaminwater reps.

"We gave away a fucking F-150 last month for top case sales and this month they bust our balls for a forty-five-cent price increase. But hey, you're welcome. I softened them up for you. You'll do great. You're the Zico guy, right? I'm Andy, love that shit."

We stood next to the door waiting to be invited in. Instead, Jerry came out and said calmly, "Mark, sorry, we'll need a few more minutes with these guys alone. You're also going to need to cut your presentation back to five minutes. That's not going to be a problem, is it?" He didn't wait for an answer before closing the door. Listening at the door, we could hear yelling and cursing and what sounded like a chair slamming to the floor. I felt like I was an extra in a Scorsese movie.

A few minutes later the little man opened the door and called out, "Zico!" I let Maura and the rest file in and I came in last. I went to the front of the packed room. Jerry introduced me over the bustle of everyone in the room talking at once. "Guys, can you please settle down and show some respect? Like I said, we'll continue this conversation tomorrow. Many of you have seen coconut water popping up on your routes and asked us to take on one of the brands. We believe this category is going to be big and that we have the best brand with the best team, and here to tell you about Zico coconut water is founder Mark Rampolla. Let's give Mark a nice welcome."

I was just about to speak, when four big guys got up in unison, noisily pushed their way down their aisle, and walked out. Three others followed. I didn't know what to do. Jerry stood up and shouted,

"Anyone else?" and paused for a minute. "Mark, please continue, so sorry about that."

I had done hundreds of speeches and spoken to audiences of five hundred or more, in foreign countries and in Spanish. But I had never been this nervous or thrown off kilter. I tried to roll with it but I would have rather spoken in front of rioting prisoners at that point. I explained what coconut water is, how we came up with the idea, how we've been selling it. I went off script and tried to end on a big note: "You guys are gonna make a ton of money off Zico, trust me," I said, trying to affect a slight New York accent that I'm sure came off like Mr. Rogers doing a Tony Soprano imitation.

I got a lukewarm round of applause as the audience shifted in their chairs. Jerry stepped back up and said, "Thank you, Mark. Guys, take it seriously, please. There's a real opportunity here. Mark and the Zico team will be handing out two free mixed cases for each route. Please take only two. Use it to seed a few of your best accounts and give this brand some attention, please."

We went out of the room. Jerry followed and said, "I'm very sorry about that. Distributor issues. Don't let it get to you. We'll do this again in a couple months."

"That didn't go well," I said to Maura afterward.

"Really?" she said sarcastically. "But I'm sure the fake New York accent won them over." Then shaking her head and exhaling, she said, "Whew, tough crowd. But Mark, next time try to just be yourself."

Why was I so nervous? Was it that the guys walked out or looked like they might throw me in the river if they didn't like Zico? Or maybe because I knew, and worried they might find out, that my posturing about Zico being a sure thing was just that? The truth was that Zico was barely still in business.

I had told my investors before the Fancy Food Show that Zico could gross $400,000 in sales during that remaining half of 2004. In the end, we had sold only four thousand cases during that time, at an average price of about $12 per case, bringing in a whopping $51,290 in sales. The total cost of the product landed in the U.S. was about $6 per case so that meant that we had a "gross margin" of maybe $25,000. That didn't come anywhere close to covering our sales team, office expenses, legal fees, accounting, and distribution and marketing expenses.

I clearly would not be able to pay myself the salary I had negotiated with the investors at our meeting in El Salvador, or anywhere close to it, making our family financial situation shaky. If sales improved, I might be able to pay myself enough to cover our mortgage and some basic expenses. When I received our personal American Express bill that November and saw we owed $2,300, I told Maura we had to cut back. She grabbed the bill, scanned it, and said, "Mark, look, there's groceries, car payments, insurance, phone and Internet, stuff for the house we both agreed we needed, and some clothes and snow boots for the girls." Then she handed me back the bill and asked, "What do you want me to cut?" We were so desperate that the few thousand dollars we expected to receive from the sale of Maura's car in El Salvador would help us tremendously. I also got a notice that due to our failure to repay the money I borrowed from my 401(k) the previous year it would be treated as taxable income, bumping up our looming tax bill.

And here we were; this was supposed to be our big break—the big leagues. But until Big Geyser sold and paid us for their first allotment of five thousand cases, we were deep in the red. It was our big spring launch but I wasn't sure we'd still be in business come summer.

Driving home with Maura we had a lot to talk about. A year and a half before, I was running a $100 million business spanning twenty countries with over three hundred employees. We had a beautiful home in San Salvador. I was making over $300,000 per year; we were saving lots of money and could still afford fabulous help, luxurious vacations, and had money left over to make a difference in the lives of others, both through volunteering and donating money to good causes. Now I was posturing like an idiot in front of a room full of sharks while behind the scenes we were teetering on the brink of bankruptcy. Is this what it meant to be an entrepreneur?

FOLLOW THE YOGIS

After my disastrous speech to the Big Geyser route owners, I quickly realized that the Geyser contract alone wasn't going to be Zico's break-through moment. After our spring "launch" everyone at Big Geyser, from the top management on down to the route owners, told me they weren't going to go out of their way to make Zico a success. Until I proved beyond a doubt that store owners were going to stock the brand and that people were actually interested in buying and drink-ing it, I was just some wannabe entrepreneur who was getting in their way.

Building the brand was my job and—as much as I would have loved a sudden increase in sales—Big Geyser was actually doing me a favor by reminding me of this fact. If your brand communicates per-sonal meaning, turning it over to someone else, especially a distribu-tion business, isn't going to work. Early on it's critical that you find the people who understand the meaning your product and brand embod-ies. You don't just want customers; you want converts.

When we conceived of Zico, we had in mind consumers who would not just buy our beverage but become our brand fanatics. So who were they? Of course I had my Google alerts set so that anytime anyone mentioned the word "Zico" on the Internet, I'd get an e-mail notification. If I needed my spirits lifted, clicking on those links would always do the trick. Zico was building a great reputation on blogs devoted to yoga, running, health, and better living in general. Watching the blog posts and the comments they elicited, I could witness in real time consumers sharing information and trying to figure out what Zico was all about.

"I have recently become hooked on coconut water. It has a very light and refreshing taste and more potassium than a banana," wrote a blogger who called himself NYnerd. "All over the tropics people drink coconut water every day, but here in New York it's very new on the scene. You heard it here first, Zico is the next Snapple." I might have been the only reader of NYnerd's blog, but I can't tell you how a personal plug like that boosted my spirits.

Zico wasn't an easy sell in many settings and it wasn't the sort of product that you could expect to gain momentum by simply putting it on random store shelves. I knew this from having spent days in the aisles of Costcos around the Tri-state Area as part of a failed Road Show, as they called it, pouring out samples of Zico. It would take five years for that spark to take. Selling to suburbanites who had carts filled with Coke six-packs and cases of beer wasn't going to work immediately.

In other settings, however, our message seemed to resonate: Zico was a natural sports drink packed with electrolytes and the perfect form of post-workout (or night out) replenishment. The triathletes, who are notoriously obsessed with what they put into their highly toned bodies, were at first suspicious of the free Zico we tried to hand them at the end of their races. But after only a few of these events, herds of racers followed the winners right up to our tent after they crossed the finish line and asked where they could buy more for their daily workout.

When I talked to the yogis and people who managed yoga studios, especially hot yoga, Zico was an easy sell. Bikram yoga, which was becoming increasingly popular, offered a challenging routine of twenty-six poses over ninety minutes in studios where the temperature was cranked to 104 degrees with 40 percent humidity. You finish these sessions dehydrated and deeply thirsty. Studios stocked crossover sports drinks like Vitaminwater, but they generally didn't like the idea of selling their customers a big dose of sugar after a workout intended to improve bodies and calm minds. That Zico was a balanced and natural way to rehydrate seemed especially relevant to Bikram students.

The yoga clientele is where I first got the sense that Zico had its own momentum—that there were other people out there advocating for the brand. At the time, a few hundred hot yoga studios existed across the country, mainly in hip, urban communities that Whole Foods was also targeting. In many of the studios, Zico was taking the place of Vitaminwater as the go-to after-class drink. So I figured building a passionate base of consumers in the yoga studios would help when we expanded into Whole Foods by creating an existing base of awareness and interest in our brand.

One day I got a call from the manager of a Bikram studio in San Francisco. He told me that some of his clients were from New York and that after classes they'd ask him how he could run a hot yoga studio without selling Zico. What exactly was this Zico stuff, he wanted to know, and how could he get some? So I began to do a healthy business shipping to Bikram studios in major metropolitan areas.

To get to know these customers better, I began to take Bikram classes around New York. The demographic was a marketer's dream: the clientele were in their mid-twenties to mid-forties, fit, and if the labels on their tote bags were any indication, fairly well-to-do. I also had the gut feeling that I was surrounded by early adopters; they were cultural leaders, who were the first to try something new, and had already brought other major brands into prominence. Lululemon, to take the best example, had appealed to this same demographic and was on its way to be a billion-dollar brand selling yoga wear. Watching these yogis buy Zicos for each other and guzzle them, often in one long gulp, made me certain that these were our brand's potential fanatics. Here was an audience that reflected what we had built Zico to represent: people intent on taking personal responsibility for their spiritual, mental, and physical health through hard work and developing a personal understanding of their natural selves.

The obvious passion this population had for Zico had more value than the sales it generated. Not only were they acting as brand ambassadors, each yoga studio also became a pin in the map indicating the geographic areas that would be most receptive to Zico. Once we sold into the yoga studio, the next stop was the bodega on the corner and then the one down the street. With this knowledge about our core consumers—our potential brand partners—I had a new way to approach and utilize our partnership with Big Geyser.

CLIMBING UP IN THE WORLD

The traditional way to get the attention of the Big Geyser route owners was basically to bribe them—or rather "incentivize" them with big prizes like that Ford F-150 that Vitaminwater had offered. Given that Maura and I were worried about how we were going to make our own car payments, that sort of incentive wasn't an option for us.

Instead, I decided to focus on the route owners that delivered to the neighborhoods with the yoga studios in which we had already made headway. I started with just three Big Geyser distributors. They all had their nickname they went by: Johnny One Drop, Mike Matco, and Steve LES (which stood for Lower East Side). Not coincidentally, these were also the only three drivers who would give me the time of day after my disastrous kickoff speech at Big Geyser. I asked each one of them if I could spend some time with them to get to know their routes.

I worked on getting to know Steve, who owned the Big Geyser route that covered a yoga-heavy part of the Lower East Side. He had two drivers making deliveries and stocking shelves, while he focused on making sales and personally checking in on his retailers. He wasn't much on making small talk but after a number of attempts, he let me ride with him as he checked in on each of the stores in his neighborhood.

"So you want to hit some Hispanic markets?" he asked me as we drove out of the Big Geyser lot on the first morning. "Zico's an ethnic play, right?" By the time we had reached lower Manhattan, I had convinced him that we were starting with a much different clientele. I pointed out the yoga studios along his route where Zico was selling well and told him that he could sell the brand in much the same way he was selling Vitaminwater. The only difference was that Zico was healthier.

"Okay," he said. "I get it. I know the sort of places where the yoga chicks shop."

A half hour later he was introducing me to the manager of a high-end corner bodega that had an Odwalla cooler and offered a variety of fresh organic fruits and vegetables. I made my pitch while he went to check the other brands he stocked. I offered the manager a special first-month deal of buying three cases and getting the fourth free. The manager hedged and then asked to think about it.

As he was about to turn away, Steve stepped to my side and took over. "Here's what Mark is going to do," he said, regaining the manager's attention. "Tomorrow he's going to show up at seven a.m. with a free case of Zico. Make that two free cases. He'll stock it himself, make it look all pretty. If it sells, you reorder. What do you got to lose?"

"Sure, okay," the manager said. "See you tomorrow."

"Thanks a ton, Steve," I said when we were back on the sidewalk. "Not only are you giving away Zico, you're having me deliver it."

"Look, Mark," he said not unkindly. "This is what it's going to take to get going. The reason you are going to deliver it yourself is that you are the best salesman for your product at this point. You are going to get to know these guys. Besides, if you give Big Geyser route owners free product to give out, they are just gonna sell those extra cases at a discount and pocket the money. Even my drivers are going to do that. It's free money to them. To make it in this business you are going to have to . . ."

"I know," I interrupted, "give until it hurts."

"Right! And then give some more," Steve laughed. "Big Hal taught you well."

So for a few months in the summer of 2005, I had my feet in two worlds, learning as much as I could about both. One day I'd be riding along with the rough-and-tumble Big Geyser route owners and the next morning I'd be sweating it out among the upper-income yoga students. I remember one of those classes that spring with crystal clarity. It was the end of the week and I showed up already pretty beat from the early morning ride-along from the day before—a condition made worse by having shared a bottle of wine with Maura the night before. The 104-degree studio felt like summer in Death Valley and I struggled through the poses trying not to tip myself or anyone around me over.

Finally, the teacher led the class into the final move: Savasana, or dead man pose. Basically you are just lying on your back relaxing. I can do this pose. "Let the work you've done do its work on your body and mind," the teacher said in a soothing voice. "Relax your head. Your eyes. Your shoulders. Your arms. Your legs. Just sink into the earth. Know that nothing else matters. You are connected with the universe. It's all okay. There will be time for stresses and problems but that time is not now. Take this last three minutes and know at the end of that you'll feel refreshed, renewed, and can face anything, and of course finally have that Zico you've been craving all class."

CHAPTER 7
BOTTLE IT UP

ONE STEP FORWARD, TWO BACK

If we only needed to work hard to make Zico a success, we'd certainly have been in the black by the end of 2005. We had made progress on several fronts but we hadn't broken through or built up the sort of momentum that would get us over (or even close to) the hump of our expenses. My strategy of building relationships with a few Big Geyser route owners at a time was working, but progress was frustratingly slow. When we focused on the neighborhoods with Bikram studios and took the time to educate the route owners, sales really picked up. But that hands-on approach was time intensive. On a one-to-one level, we could almost always convince a store owner, driver, or customer of the value of Zico but with just a couple of us, this method was hard to scale. On the positive side, by the summer of 2005 sales had doubled at Big Geyser. But that was only from 500 cases per month at the end of 2004 to just over 1,000 cases a month by late summer 2005—around $12,000 in sales per month. Depending on which side of the bed I got out on, that was either the start of exponential growth or a pathetic number that I could practically drink with a few friends.

Getting the route owners in Big Geyser's network to embrace Zico enthusiastically remained elusive. Most days of the week, I'd get up at four a.m. and, after a run, drive to the distribution center to try to chat up the route owners and get a sense for how I could help them sell more Zico into their accounts. I'd put on my best game face when I walked into the warehouse and come out feeling beaten up. If I even got to talk to them it was often: "I need more free samples." "Your display at that deli on Lexington looks like shit." "No, I don't need another fucking T-shirt." "Your price is too high." "Those Vita Coco guys are kicking your ass." These guys gave new meaning to the word tough.

I had taken Hal's advice to "give until it hurts, then give some more" to heart. I gave distributors a constant supply of free cases but it never seemed to be enough. I was also learning about the dark side of the beverage distribution system. I'd hear about some accounts paying $18 per case of Zico, not the $15.99 it was supposed to be. The "deals" we gave at that time were buy five cases get one free and buy ten get three free and sometimes buy twenty get five free. They were supposed to be linked to an individual account to build customer loyalty and encourage higher volume orders. But when I talked to retailers, I learned that some distributors would take the free cases and simply sell them to other accounts.

These weren't the type of guys you wanted to call out even if you knew they were taking advantage of you. A few times early on I had complained to Big Geyser about the way Zico was displayed or being sold into accounts, only to later get a dirty stare and the cold shoulder from the offending parties. It was prison yard rules: no crime worse than being a rat. I learned that I had to deal with distributors directly and if I had an issue to iron it out with them personally. As I got to know more of them I could see that they were mostly good guys trying to make a buck in the brutally tough daily grind of New York City retail. But "give until it hurt" was still the mantra of the day and, man, did it hurt.

Zico was still getting good press and we had a growing base of loyal customers. That momentum, little as it was, had opened up the possibility of dozens of potential pathways and partnerships for growth. I had received inquiries from distributors in Massachusetts, Indianapolis, Austin, San Francisco, Barbados, and even one in Korea. The Vitamin Shoppe had asked about carrying Zico, and every week I'd get a call from another yoga studio that wanted me to ship them some cases. Zico was one of the first beverages ever carried by Amazon.com and sales were showing steady growth as well, although the whole Amazon food initiative was still in its infancy.

I was faced with what scientists call a signal-to-noise ratio. I had an ever-increasing amount of data about how consumers, retailers, and distributors were reacting to Zico, but it was difficult to determine how much was useful and *potentially actionable* information and how much was just random noise.

The only real way to figure out what would work was to experiment with my options. I basically needed to place bets with my effort and time and find out which ones would pay off. Distributing through United Natural Foods (UNFI), for instance, looked like it was worth the gamble. They were the major player in the natural foods industry and primary distributor for Whole Foods nationwide.

After some negotiating, UNFI ordered five hundred cases for their warehouse in New England, which was outside of the Big Geyser territory. It was a six-thousand-dollar sale. Not bad for a first order. They had dozens of distribution centers around the country and once again, I couldn't keep my mind from doing the math of how that could quickly add up. Two months later, I got a check for a little over two thousand dollars and a two-page list of the deductions for retailer discounts, manufacturers' charge backs, promotions, and damaged or unsellable product. I was beginning to realize Big Hal's lesson would apply outside of New York as well.

Distributors weren't the only ones playing for every advantage. Retailers had their own demands and schemes. They'd want a "free fill," basically free cases to begin to carry Zico, and sometimes request "slotting fees," basically cash in exchange for shelf space. Sometimes they'd take the liberty to discount the price of Zico and deduct the amount they'd pay me or the distributor (which would be charged back to me). Of course, no one ever paid us more if they decided to bump the price up, which happened often. We'd see 12-ounce cartons of Zico selling for $3.50 or $4.00 in some accounts when it was supposed to be at $1.99.

At the time I felt like the world was against me and that the cost of doing business might actually put me out of business. But looking back now I can see these businesses were doing what they needed to do to manage the hundreds, even thousands, of upstart brands and survive themselves. Further, these experiences were actually the cost of *learning* this business. So I had to understand the potential pitfalls and not fall into them, or at least not fall into them twice. My learning curve during those years was steep and very expensive, but the street-level knowledge I gained would be incredibly helpful when we grew and had dozens of employees managing as many distributors with millions of dollars in sales and expenses.

CASH IS KING

During business school I learned about cash flow, but I frankly didn't really get it then. I would argue that it's the single most important concept in business, especially for start-ups. Tracking weekly or monthly sales is important and fun, but a new business lives or dies by its ability to generate cash. In fact, one of the most common ways strong, growing early businesses falter is the failure to understand and manage cash flow. If sales are growing quickly but you get paid in thirty or sixty or ninety days, how do you keep up with ordering or producing more product? That often creates a cash crisis for many growing businesses.

I'd started to grasp cash flow by running International Paper's businesses in Latin America, where I had to generate cash in each stand-alone foreign business to pay dividends at the end of the year. But those businesses were mature, profitable, slow growing, and I had a team of finance and operations people to manage all the details.

Zico's cash flow cycle, on the other hand, was like juggling knives. On the supply side, let's say I ordered a full forty-foot container load of product, which was the most economical unit to produce and ship from Brazil. The cost of those 5,500 cases was roughly $22,000. Add on shipping and importation charges, call it $25,000 to have it sitting in our New Jersey warehouse. I needed to pay Amacoco 50 percent up front when I placed an order so they could buy the packaging and the next crop of coconuts. A month after that, they'd put my order into production and then wait ten days to make sure the product had no microbiological issues. They expected payment in full before it shipped out of their warehouses. A month after that, the cases would show up in a port in New Jersey where they could be held by customs for another two weeks. I never wanted to run out of product (especially given the risk of delays importing from Brazil), so I always wanted to have at least one month of inventory on hand. So those 5,500 cases would sit in the warehouse for a month while we sold product from the previous month. Then we would start to sell from this shipment. Big Geyser wanted to carry the least amount of inventory possible, so they would order small amounts twice a week; same with Amazon.

Our customers agreed to pay us thirty days from when they

received the product, but we were lucky to get paid in forty-five days. Add all that up and I was looking at a four-month cash-to-cash cycle, recouping $48,000 (after deductions, discounts, and all the free product, we never received the full $60,000 we invoiced) four months after I made the first payment for the product.

Here's the problem that illustrates why even profitable businesses can fail when they don't have cash on hand: We were growing, year over year, but the monthly income was wildly variable. The prime beverage season was April through October, with June through August being the cash cows. So $55,000 might come in one month, and only $17,000 a few months later. Expenses were variable as well. If I needed to get ready for a big summer promotion, I'd have to order five containers in late winter or early spring, which were bad months for income. I'd also have weekly and monthly expenses that couldn't be put off, including paying employees, rent, warehouse fees, insurance, and more (collectively my burn rate). There are ways to solve this cash flow problem with supplier financing, bank loans, payment terms, receivable factoring, etc. But these solutions are rarely available to small start-ups without hefty up-front costs or usurious interest rates.

I was constantly trying to balance cash flow and supply two or three months into the future with a bunch of unknowns. If not enough money came in, I couldn't pay my Amacoco bill to get the product on the boats headed to the U.S. Pallets of Zico would sit in their shipping facility while I scrambled to get distributors and retailers to pay their bills. If I ordered too much, I'd be stuck with extra warehousing bills and product that might not sell by its expiration date.

By the end of the summer of 2005, we were gaining a little traction, and the good news was that Zico was selling well, and velocity (the rate of sales per outlet) in yoga studios, natural food stores, and small shops was strong and growing. We were also gaining new accounts every week. The problem was that it all just wasn't happening fast enough. We were up to about $20,000 per month in sales when we needed double that to begin to see black. The $500,000 we had raised from existing investors at the beginning of the year was depleting quickly, and I would have to look hard yet again at reducing all expenses and finding new investment capital.

When Maura asked how the business was going, I often reported to her all the sales we had made on paper—not what we actually had in the bank. It wasn't long before she caught on to my all-too-optimistic accounting and began to realize we were not only not out of the woods yet, we were just beginning to get to the deepest, darkest parts.

OUR FIRST RESIGNATION

Maura had been intimately involved with Zico from the beginning but did not have an official job title or set of responsibilities or salary. Basically she jumped in where needed. In 2003 and 2004 between breast-feedings, she eagerly researched and worked on the original business plan with me. When I was traveling for IP, she was the point person for everything, including following up with team members on their parts of the R & D process. She shopped for wearables and giveaways, helped with packaging, copy, and messaging. She worked the trade shows. She was a great sounding board for me with strategy, investor reports, and priorities. She has this knack for remembering details and conversations I sometimes conveniently forgot (or tried to forget). She was my biggest fan but would always give it to me straight—sometimes to my chagrin.

In late 2004, I asked her to be in charge of a few specific roles more officially: public relations, events, and coordinating demos. We could not afford to continue to retain the public relations firm we were paying $5,000 per month. So I made Maura the offer that Zico would hire her at $3,000 per month and she could work completely flexible hours, but she would get paid at some future date. Look at the bright side, I said, you won't have to pay much in taxes for a few years.

She agreed to take the job and she was great. She found the right events and got us into them and she continued to generate good press. She scheduled samplings at stores, often staffing the table herself. She, Roberto, and Jose got along famously and complemented each other's skills. We had a few disagreements here and there but I thought we were working through it well. I tried to treat her like other employees, at least during team meetings. I was tough with everyone: I had high expectations and welcomed all feedback but made my own decisions. Going to events together, having lunch together some days, talking strategy, celebrating new sales, and sharing the burden of the frequent setbacks were fun to do together. But our "pillow talk" now often became about warehouse fees and customs forms that needed to be filled out. Talk about a mood killer. Before she was giving her opinion, advice, or serving as a sounding board for me from the outside; we were figuring it out together as a team. Now she was reporting to me and I struggled with how to hear her opinion and input relative to Jose and Roberto and respect everyone as equals. She did not enjoy or embrace being managed by me. Our marriage was predicated on equality, but in business I had the last word.

One Saturday evening in the fall of 2005, Maura pulled into the driveway after running a promotion at the finish line of a race. We were tag teaming that weekend so she covered that event and I had one in Montauk, on the eastern tip of Long Island, early the following morning.

"Hi. How'd it go?" I asked.

"Fine," she said. "Runners were loving Zico, spectators about fifty-fifty." I waited to hear more but she was unusually silent.

"Could you finish unpacking this stuff?" She exhaled, already turning toward the house. "I'm exhausted and I haven't seen the girls all weekend. By the way, your truck is totally out of alignment and fishtails on the highway. I'm not driving that thing again until you get it fixed and neither should you. And the pop-up tent is broken. We need better ones."

I took out the barrel coolers and turned them upside down on the driveway to drain, and rearranged a few loose T-shirts and pamphlets. I'd be driving the same electric-blue five-year-old Nissan Pathfinder two hundred miles round-trip for the Montauk triathlon in the morning, so I loaded it up with cases until it could pass as a low rider.

When I finished I went into the house. The girls were playing downstairs but Maura was nowhere in sight. I found her sitting silently on our bed upstairs. From the way she held her shoulders, I could tell something was very wrong.

"You okay?" I asked from the doorway. When she began to cry I knew the answer.

"Mark, I can't do this," she said in between sobs. "I'm resigning from Zico. Zico is a great product, I believe in the vision and will continue to support you. It's just too much. We only talk about work. You're always stressed and me working with you, *for you*, basically doubles the pressure on both of us. And we need some outside income so that we can pay our bills."

I wish I could tell you that my initial reaction was calm understanding and reassurance. What I actually said was: "You've got to be fucking kidding me. You can't quit."

The formality of the word "resigning" angered me. She wasn't resigning, she was bailing, abandoning me on a sinking ship, deserting me in the midst of battle!

She handed me a piece of paper she was holding. Holy cow, I thought, she's written up a formal resignation letter! Then I recognized the document as the original screens we had made when evaluating business ideas. They specified our hopes for the venture but more importantly, they listed some nonnegotiable items. We promised each other that we'd maintain our health and our integrity, that we'd bring the world a healthy product, and that we'd be honest with those investors and employees who partnered with us. The last item on the page was underlined. We promised each other that we would not let starting a business endanger our marriage.

"I believe in you and don't want you to feel I'm bailing on you," she said, still in tears. "This is so hard for me to say. Mark, no business is worth risking our marriage. We swore to each other that we wouldn't let that happen. Now is the time to come through on that promise." Her voice conveyed no anger or accusation. She was simply stating a very difficult fact that I—in my overly optimistic style—had been avoiding for months.

My feelings of abandonment didn't magically disappear but Maura's forthrightness and honesty began to sink in. There was a long silence as she allowed me to think through what she had said.

"I get it," I said, sitting down next to her on the bed. "I can only imagine how hard this was for you to say." She started to cry again as I pulled her close, but this time there was some relief in the sobs.

"Mark, I'm not quitting you," she said. "I'm leaving the day-to-day at Zico. I still want to be involved. And actually when we first started out we agreed I'd help launch it and work in it for about eighteen months until we got off the ground. We need reliable income *now*, not in three years when Zico might be able to pay me. There is a maternal- and child-health nonprofit nearby. They need someone to develop a curriculum to help low-income women have healthy pregnancies. It's totally up my alley and the pay is decent for a nonprofit."

"Yeah, that does make sense." I sighed. "Let's go make dinner for the girls and not say another word about Zico. Let's open a nice bottle of wine."

"It might be a good time to open one of the moments we've bottled up," she said. I understood what she meant right away. Often in moments of special joy we'd turn to each other and say bottle it up, we might need to tap into this when things get tough. Before Zico we had done a lot of bottling but rarely dipped into the cellar.

"Which one should we open?" I asked.

"Maybe that first time we took both girls to Tesoro Beach in El Salvador," she said. "Let's have some of that one." She smiled as I made my best attempt to make the sound of a cork popping from a champagne bottle. "The sound of heaven as my dad would say." She grinned.

I've seen many romantic partners found and operate businesses together. Some are wildly successful: Janie and Lance Hoffman from Mamma Chia, for example. In my personal experience, however, it rarely works out on the business or couple fronts, especially with children in the mix. I am not a fan of couples businesses and I can assure you it's a red flag for most smart investors. It can work but it's tough.

Simply put, Zico would not exist or be what it is today without Maura. She played a critical role. But we both agreed our relationship was nonnegotiable and her stepping away from the day-to-day operations probably saved our marriage and was certainly best for our girls. I also believe it helped us make Zico even more of a force; she continued to make a major contribution to Zico's ultimate success and allowed us to win as a couple. But at the time, her resigning was a low point. Unfortunately, things would get worse before they got better.

THE INCREDIBLE SHRINKING COMPANY

So the small staff of Zico was reduced by one and, sadly for the company's finances, Maura was the only employee besides myself willing to defer salary into the indefinite future. Our team at the time included me; Roberto and Jose, who worked 50 percent of their time as consultants to Zico (Roberto on sales and Jose on marketing); Juan, who managed the back office, took orders, manned the phones, and did whatever else was necessary; Chris, who was our first sales hire in 2004 and managed half of Big Geyser's territory; James, whom we had hired at the beginning of the summer to be a counterpart to Chris and manage the other half; and Jhonnie, who worked part-time dropping off product, driving the van for demos and events, and was himself developing into a solid salesman occasionally calling on accounts on sales blitzes or route rides.

As 2005 came to a close, I recognized that I was going to have to cut back even further. Worse still, summer was over and with it the hot and humid months when people spend a little extra money to quench their thirst. Even though those Bikram studios would still be cranking out the heat, our growth would likely slow in the winter—maybe even decline—and Zico couldn't live on sales to Bikram yoga studios alone.

It wasn't for lack of effort that sales were not taking off. That year, 2005, we had displayed Zico at Fancy Food Shows in San Francisco and Chicago and at Expo East in Baltimore. We had taken meetings with twenty-one major retail accounts from ShopRite to Costco. We met with a dozen brokers (sales agents that would represent Zico when selling into larger chain retailers) and signed seven to represent the brand. We met with fifty-six distributors across natural, beverage, specialty, and sports channels. And we had been contacted by potential distributors in Australia, the UK, Singapore, Spain, Germany, China, Taiwan, Japan, India, Argentina, Denmark, Thailand, Jamaica, Costa Rica, Canada, El Salvador, the Bahamas, Barbados, Dominican Republic, and France. This in addition to hundreds of account calls in New York and giving away thousands of cases at demos

and events. I also personally had discussions with at least fifty potential investors. But despite all that, none of it was happening fast
enough.

All told our payroll was about $24,000 per month plus another
$2,300 for rent. Everyone was being paid well below market, espe-
cially Roberto, Jose, and me. But even so, our monthly burn rate, which
averaged out to about $60,000, was still too high given our level of
sales and the capital we had raised.

I calculated that I needed to get our total monthly expenses to
under $25,000 if we were going to be able to survive the winter and
have more time to find new investors and grow sales.

In early October 2005, I had a meeting with Roberto and Jose in
the small conference room of the office we shared. They had both quit
good full-time jobs to start their own marketing and advertising firm,
and Zico was their principal client. Roberto was an investor and both
had earned equity in Zico. But we had been clear from the beginning
that their continued engagement was based on us achieving certain
sales targets, and the unavoidable truth was that we were at a fraction
of what we had predicted.

"Guys, look, I want to cut to the chase," I told them after we got
seated. "We are not in a good situation, and I need to take some drastic measures to keep the company afloat through the winter. I need to
cancel our contract and move out of the office. I'm also going to let go
of everyone but Chris. I'll respect the thirty-day clause in our contract
and pay you rent for that period and you'll still have the equity you
earned in Zico, but believe me, I'm doing this so it's worth something
someday. I don't blame you. I was not realistic about what it would
take to get this business off the ground and how much I didn't know
about this industry."

"Look, Mark," Roberto said with a sigh, "we had a feeling this was
coming and have already talked about it. We totally understand and

feel terrible ourselves that we were not able to generate the level of sales we hoped. Don't worry about the last month. We'll figure it out. Keep every penny in Zico and keep at it. Continue to use the office as long as you need to get settled somewhere else. We want you to win! By the way, can you really find something cheaper than this?"

"Yup," I said. "It's at 435 Grant Avenue, Suite A, otherwise known as my garage. I'm going to redo the loft space above and that will be the new world headquarters for Zico."

"We love Zico and you and Maura so we will do anything we can to help," Jose said. "Just let us know. And if you have to pull some stuff off the shelves that doesn't make its sell-by date, drop it by the office. I'm now so addicted to Zico, I'm afraid to live without it!"

"Unfortunately, but fortunately for you, we are swimming in product so you can drink and share what you want. Please get more people addicted. That's what we need."

That same day I gathered Juan, James, and Jhonnie together. I explained what was happening and about my conversation with Roberto and Jose. I said I needed to let them all go. Again I told them that it was nothing they did and that the blame was squarely on me. I told them I'd pay them the two-week severance that was in their contract, plus an extra month so they could transition while looking for other jobs, and that I would be happy to give them all strong references.

Maura was sick about this. Somehow the excitement of a year ago and the expanding of staff were so short-lived. It physically pained Maura and she felt we had let our team down. I wasn't just having to cut jobs at a company. I was having to live with decisions I made for *our* company, having to change course, and letting go of individuals who were not only employees and contractors, but friends.

In general, our team took the setback better than I did. The economy was still strong (actually radically overheated as we would soon learn) and they all had new jobs within weeks. They were on to new challenges while I was left with the sense that I had failed them, Maura, and myself.

The Zico team now consisted of two, Chris and me, working at our "global headquarters." Chris was the only one I had hired who had any real beverage experience prior to Zico as a salesman for New York's largest beer distributor. He had taught me a lot and could handle himself at Geyser, which was what I really needed.

We now had a rent-free garage office and total expenses of less than $25,000 per month. At a minimum we needed an additional investment infusion of $300,000 to get through the next year. After placing some orders for more Zico to get us ready for the spring, we were down to $50,000 cash and some accounts receivable but were owed more than that to vendors. Technically bankrupt yet again.

I had warned our investors in December of 2005 that things didn't look good, so in January 2006 I arranged a conference call with all of them to explain what needed to happen. I told them the whole story—the good, the bad, and the ugly—and took responsibility for not achieving what I had planned. Within a few days, the core group of investors came through for the third time with $300,000 at only a slight increase in valuation from the initial financing round. With this infusion our ownership stake fell yet again, to below 40 percent.

I still believed in coconut water and in Zico and knew that we really needed $1 to $2 million to even begin to capitalize on the opportunity just in New York alone, but $300,000 would have to do. And being lean and mean allowed me to breathe a little on the home front. Now that we had some money in the bank, I could draw a modest salary, though a fraction of what I made before. We were still very tight. Living in New Jersey was a fortune relative to El Salvador. Looked like it was Target pajamas and candy for Christmas again this year; no big presents were in our budget.

THE GARAGE

Imagine a cold New Jersey night in late March 2006. I'm in the garage of our family home packing up cases of Zico for shipment to Bikram and other hot yoga studios in cities I'm hoping to expand into—eventually. I personally built out the loft area of this 1920s two-car detached garage to become the global corporate headquarters for Zico, running wiring, insulating the rafters, laying the floor, hanging drywall, building desks, painting, etc. The lower part, where we used to park our cars and store bikes and camping gear, is now packed to the rafters with pallets of Zico, boxes of T-shirts, banners, beach balls, posters, an easy-up promotional tent, and all the pieces of our trade show booth.

Of course, working a start-up business out of a garage has some cultural credibility in America. The garages where Apple and Hewlett-Packard were founded have both been named historic landmarks. But as you grow, you're supposed to move *out of* the garage. Zico and I seemed to be going in reverse.

Dressed in an old winter coat, gloves, and a hat (did I mention that there was no heat in the bottom of Suite A?), I grab another generic brown box and expertly open and fold the seams and flip the box top down. Taping the bottom and flipping the box upright, I pack it with four cases of Zico. I add a hand-signed note card, one Zico T-shirt, a few sales brochures, and tape the top. I've often avoided bigger problems looming in the near future by simply putting my head down and just plowing forward. Tonight, I'm an automaton. No thinking. Just doing. I have this process so down I could do it in my sleep. Which is very near what I'm doing.

One problem in the beverage industry is that, no matter how economical the packaging, the product is never lightweight. Why didn't I launch dried coconut chips? It might be killing my back but in some weird way this manual labor is the best part of my day. I know exactly what to do, I can do it efficiently, and I can see tangible results. Each four-case box also represents a real sale, money that will be coming into the Zico bank account—a small countercurrent to the flood of money pouring out.

Maura comes in from the side door and calls out loud enough to be heard over the Led Zeppelin echoing around the garage. "Mark, it's nine thirty. You've been out here for hours and it's freezing. Come inside and let's sit down for a few minutes before you miss your window." Her voice sounds upbeat, or rather it is meant to sound upbeat. After ten years together I know the difference. She knows how I need to be in bed by ten p.m. so I'm up by four or four thirty. "I'm almost done," I say. "I had no idea it was so late." I look back at the stack of blue Zico cases on a wooden pallet that used to be almost shoulder high and now has only sixteen cases on it. I then look at the stack of labeled brown boxes, each packed with four cases of Zico ready to ship out tomorrow via UPS to yoga studios across the country. What was an empty pallet just a few hours ago is now almost full.

I ask Maura to give me ten minutes. I wanted to get through the rest of the pallet. "Okay," she says, "ten minutes." She knows me and knows when I get in this sort of zone I can go for hours, all night, even if it practically kills me. She first saw this side of me in grad school when I could work on watershed hydrology spreadsheets all night until I looked like a zombie. She knew I was working hard, but I'm sure she wondered if I was doing the right things. So did I. After all, was the best use of my MBA and experience from running a business with three hundred people to now be packing boxes in a garage at ten p.m.?

I plow through the remaining cases. I want to end the day with the satisfaction of packing up a whole pallet of Zico: 250 cases. That would be my personal evening record.

I finish up a half hour later—overly optimistic yet again. I turn off the music and flip off the buzzing fluorescent light. I get into the house and strip out of the dirty winter gear. The girls are long asleep and I join Maura on the living room couch in front of the fireplace. I ask her if she wants me to start a fire but she tells me not to worry about it, seeing how exhausted I am. I pour myself an Irish whiskey and we sit for a few minutes and catch up.

One of the things I loved about Maura when we met, and for the ten years we had been together since, is she is one of the most positive, happy people I've ever met. She'd even laugh at her own jokes regardless of anyone else's reaction saying, "My grandfather always said why wait to be tickled?" She isn't laughing tonight and not very often these days. I know she's depressed. She has reason to be. Heck, I probably am, too, but try not to even entertain that possibility.

Coming out of the trance of work I had put myself in, the reality of our situation begins to come back into view. Just a couple of months ago I fired all but one of the Zico staff, canceled my contract with Jose and Roberto, and moved out of the nice office we had in Englewood Cliffs, New Jersey. Despite all these cuts we are still touch and go financially, both in the business and in our personal lives. Just as I can read Maura's mood without any information being exchanged, she can read mine. "Mark," she says, "do we need to sell the house?"

Though our existing investors had contributed $300,000 at the beginning of the year, I know that is not going to last long, especially (back to the cash flow crunch) if we want to really grow. This year is going to be very tough and though Zico is gaining traction, if we have one misstep it could all fall apart. I don't want to hide this from Maura. I couldn't even if I tried.

"We might," I lament as tears stream down her face. "But we're not there yet."

STREET FIGHT

As if I didn't have enough to worry about going into the summer of 2006, the competition with Vita Coco, the coconut water brand that had appeared almost simultaneously with Zico, was getting ever more intense. Talking to store owners and others in the industry, I began to piece together exactly who I was up against.

From what I was able to gather, these guys were also outsiders to the beverage industry and, like myself, they were committed, passionate, and unconventional. I was told one of the founders, Mike Kirban, had founded a software company he still owned and could be seen most days gliding on inline skates from bodega to bodega with a backpack of Vita Coco pitching store owners. Hard not to like that sort of free-spirited dedication.

Like me, they were relatively young, ambitious, and hungry as hell. In fact, they were younger, were not married, and had no kids. I'm not sure my MBA and corporate experience gave me any advantage, and perhaps it worked against me: these guys were scrappy, and in a street fight that's sometimes all that counts. And they were clearly watching my every move. When I put up on our website the fact that each bottle of Zico contained "more potassium than a banana," Vita Coco began claiming that their drink had more potassium than *two* bananas. Our claim was factual. Their claim was also true, if you happened to have two very small bananas. On one hand, the imitation and emulation was flattering; on the other, it was a pain in the ass.

The guys behind Vita Coco seemed to have a different standard than I did when it came to being honest with consumers. In some of their early promotional materials, they suggested that coconut water could regulate intestinal function, detoxify your body, and boost your immune system and circulation. They hadn't completely pulled these supposed properties out of the air—coconut water was touted as a folk remedy in these ways in Brazil, Thailand, and Indonesia. But American consumers (and the FDA) expected such claims to be backed up with science.

These guys did have me worried. But I also felt that there were advantages to this rivalry. In fighting for publicity, retail space, and partnerships within the beverage industry, together we were raising the general awareness about coconut water. If a retailer was being pitched by two new coconut water brands, they were more likely to think that the product was worth paying attention to. The same dynamic would likely be true for investors, distributors, customers, and the behemoths of the beverage industry (like Coke and Pepsi) who might someday be looking to buy in as strategic partners or outright owners.

Of course, retailers soon figured out that they could play us against each other. "Maybe we'll put you on the shelves," I was often told by store owners, "if you can give me more free cases than that roller-skating Vita Coco guy." This was our new reality when negotiating with corner stores and major retailers alike. Buyers were pushing us to make increasingly absurd deals. If we offered a "buy ten, get two free" deal, Vita Coco would come back with "buy twenty, get five free," which would then be countered with a "buy thirty, get ten free." At this rate, we'd be giving our entire production away in a year. Zico and Vita Coco were playing a dangerous game of who could let the most blood.

FLIRTING WITH ANOTHER

In late 2006, I faced another challenge. My bestselling route owner, Steve Gross, who covered the Lower East Side of Manhattan and had shown me the ropes early on, was leaving Big Geyser to start his own independent distributorship. Knowing that few name-brand beverages would leave Big Geyser, he had to place his bets on some upstart brands he hoped to make into big sellers. He wanted Zico to be one of those brands and I was impressed by his enthusiasm and liked the idea of being a lead brand in his new business.

The problem was my ironclad contract with Big Geyser. To go with Steve, I'd have to leave Big Geyser entirely and it promised to be a bad breakup.

Steve's offer wasn't the only reason I was reconsidering leaving Big Geyser. The Whole Foods Markets in the New York area had recently begun to sell Zico, which Big Geyser was delivering. The brand was doing well enough in those area stores that the buyers at Whole Foods wanted to carry it in stores over the entire northeast region. But we faced one problem: Big Geyser didn't cover the whole northeast, so Whole Foods wanted us to use UNFI, a leading national distributor of natural, organic, and specialty foods. And that would mean any retailer could order Zico through them—including New York retailers who also had accounts with Big Geyser. Per my Big Geyser contract, if they did that, I'd start racking up $10 or $20 per case in "invasion fee" charges. I could potentially expand to test new markets, but the cost of doing so might put me out of business.

Given Big Geyser's reputation and my personal experience "negotiating" a contract with them, I didn't think there was a chance in hell they would work with me to find a solution. Figuring that I'd have to get out of my contract with Big Geyser regardless, I needed to know that I had a plan B before I told them the news.

Steve and his new distributorship, Exclusive Beverages, was my plan B. The contract he offered me was much less restrictive than the one I had with Big Geyser. For Steve, I'd be a bigger fish (at least relative to the size of the pond). Steve and I kept our negotiations secret. I wasn't going to sit down with Big Geyser unless I knew exactly where I stood.

Finally, I met with Big Geyser to tell them I was leaving. In the meeting with Lewis, I explained that Whole Foods was a critical place to grow the Zico brand—the exact audience to become brand ambassadors to help spread to other markets. I wanted to keep building the brand in New York but the restrictions on my Big Geyser contract were making regional growth impossible.

"So here's the deal," I said as confidently as I could manage, "I'm going to have to get out of the contract I've signed with you." I told him I understood that I'd have to buy my way out—I calculated the figure at around $75,000 given our recent sales. "I'm not happy about this and you are not going to be happy when I tell you I don't have the money to pay you now. But I'll respect the contract and we'll just have to work out some sort of terms on payment. I will pay you eventually."

I paused as Lewis thought over what I had said. I don't think he noticed that I was holding my breath. Everything I knew about these guys suggested that walking away from the contract and telling them that you'd pay them the money you owed them someday in the future wasn't going to go over well at all.

"Let's not go ballistic here," Lewis said finally. "I understand what you're saying. What if we give you a waiver for UNFI? If you can commit that they aren't going to undercut us in price, then we can live with it."

I was speechless for a moment. Here was the man who, a year before, wouldn't let me change a single comma in their ironclad contract. Now he was telling me that I could sign with another distributor who might sell into their territory? I guess the goodwill I had built up was worth something after all. It took only a single day to have a one-page revision signed by both parties.

When I told Steve that Big Geyser had given me an out and that I wasn't going to jump ship and sign with him, he took it very personally and felt that I had lied to him. The phrase, "it's just business," is often the excuse for bad behavior. But in this case, I hoped that Steve might see that I was honestly—and without malice—choosing be-tween two competing options. Nothing I could say to him seemed to matter; for Steve, my decision was a betrayal that would, he promised, be paid back in kind. About a week later, I saw the first case of Vita Coco come off one of Steve's trucks on the Lower East Side.

I realize now I should have been much more up front with Steve and set his expectations appropriately. I should have been clearer that I could not commit until after the Big Geyser meeting. Truth was, I had just not seen the possibility that Big Geyser would be flexible. As Warren Buffett once wrote to his top managers, "We can afford to lose money—even a lot of money. But we cannot afford to lose reputation—even a shred of reputation." I had lost some of mine, and was about to pay a very heavy price when Exclusive and Vita Coco joined forces to make a fantastic team of scrappy, small companies fighting the mighty Big Geyser together.

GETTING OUR MOJO BACK

We ended 2006 with $440,000 in sales and a loss of $200,000, which was a far cry from the $1 million in sales I thought we could hit. But this was double from the previous year, and Big Geyser was now dis-tributing an average of 2,000 cases per month, double as well from the previous summer. I had again failed to attract any new investors and for the fourth time my existing investors came through, though this time with only $134,000 and a sharp message: The well was dry. Any additional investment would have to come from others. But we were building strong momentum and I was determined that in 2007 we'd finally crack the elusive $1 million revenue hurdle.

Two events brought new attention to Zico in early 2007, and nei-ther had anything to do with the brand or me. On the first of February, Coke announced that it had signed a deal to purchase Fuze Beverage, maker of enhanced waters and teas, for a rumored $250 million. Fuze wasn't in the coconut water business, but they were definitely in the New Age beverage category and the deal proved that the big beverage companies were seriously worried about all the upstart brands that were chipping away at their soda sales. A few months later, Coke struck again with their purchase of Glacéau, the maker of Vitaminwater, this time for over $4 billion. The remarkable price tag was not based strictly on earnings but more for the company's perceived potential. The price-to-sales ratio was astounding unless you were assuming that Vitaminwater's upward trajectory would continue basically forever.

After the sale was announced, the *New York Times* ran a major business article with this lead: "If you set up a lemonade stand this weekend, you might consider stirring in something a little different . . . As American consumers shift away from soda, there is a growing demand for innovative beverages, particularly if they offer health benefits." The Coke purchase of Glacéau, the article went on, "offered the most compelling evidence yet that coming up with a new beverage, or putting a new twist on an old one, can be lucrative."

That deal definitely got people's attention and sent the unmistakable message that there was gold in them there hills—new beverage brands could be worth fortunes. Who would be next? A few months later Vita Coco announced it had sold 20 percent of its company to a prominent, deep-pocketed venture firm out of Europe called Verlinvest for $2 million.

If I was going to catch this wave of interest, now was time to step it up. With the amount of money perceived to be available, opportunities opened up. I was able to recruit some very respected players in the industry to form a board of advisors for Zico, including Jim Tonkin, who had literally grown up in the beverage industry as the son of a bottler (sometimes affectionately called SOBs) and was a consultant for numerous beverage start-ups; and Jack Belsito, the former president of Snapple I had met through some industry connections.

The summer of 2007 brought strong gains on all fronts, and it was just in time. Vita Coco was making great strides with its new partnership with Exclusive and spending that money they raised on getting more and better distribution in New York. Just weeks after Maura and I had seeded numerous key Hamptons accounts, Vita Coco followed on our heels offering outlandish giveaway deals to try to muscle us out of our precious yoga studios and new retailers. Every beverage shelf I turned to seemed to be sporting containers of Vita Coco. The battle was definitely on.

BIG GEYSER MEETING

Despite the excited industry buzz over which new beverages might follow in Vitaminwater's wake and the strong traction we had developed over the summer, I was still struggling to get the full attention of Big Geyser and their route owners. In October of 2007, I couldn't even get a five-minute speaking slot at their monthly sales meeting. I asked Jerry Reda, the Big Geyser COO at the time who coordinated the meetings, and all I got was, "Mark, not this month but definitely in the spring." I'd been getting this sort of brush-off for two years and counting.

I attended the meeting anyway, just to show my face and hopefully get a chance to talk to some of the guys informally and of course to give away some more free cases. On my way out of the building I ran into Lewis Hershkowitz. He said, "Mark, good to see you. I like what I'm seeing from Zico. I'd like to sit down with you, Jerry, and Dan, so please come to my office in about forty-five minutes." Lewis was in the process of taking over the operation from his dad and if he wanted to meet, I was going to be there. An hour later, I was ushered into Lewis's office by his assistant. In the room, I saw Jerry Reda, Dan Reade, who reported to Jerry and ran the five boroughs and was a big Zico fan, and Steven, Lewis's brother who ran customer service and also believed in Zico.

"Mark, great to see you," said Lewis, looking up from a spreadsheet. "Take a seat, we're just trying to figure out what the hell is going on with Zico."

He looked back down at the documents on his desk and paused. "So," he said, "who the hell is buying all this crap?"

I opened my mouth to speak but when Lewis looked up, he was directing the question to Jerry.

"Well, we're doing decent volume each month with a positive upward trend," he began, looking at his own copy of the spreadsheet. "Some drivers are killing it, but others haven't sold a single case. It's doing well in Fairway and numbers are up at Whole Foods. It did well in the Hamptons this summer, too."

"I can see that," Lewis interrupted. "What I want to know is who is buying this shit and why? We're selling over four thousand cases per month versus two thousand last summer and one thousand the summer before. Zico is our fastest-growing brand. Who the fuck is drinking all that coconut water? Plus, from what I hear, Vita Coco is doing almost as well. If we can keep it growing at this rate, that's a real business and could even become a whole new category, but we have to know what's working and why."

They went back and forth for a few minutes between Jerry, Lewis, Dan, and Steven, but no one had a complete picture.

"Excuse me, gentlemen," I finally interrupted. "Would you like me to tell you who's buying all this 'shit' and why?" I said, holding up a Zico carton.

They all looked up at me as though they'd forgotten I was in the room. "Okay, Mark," Lewis said, "we're all ears."

"Lewis," I began, "you told me we needed to build this brand ourselves for a while. Jerry, you said to pick a couple route owners and win with them. Dan, you told me which accounts really mattered, and Steven, you always said we needed to find the right consumer base. Guys, I followed the playbook you outlined!"

I then went on a ten-minute explanation about what strategy we followed. I told them about starting with the Bikram yoga studios. I told them how we worked with the route owners who serviced those studios and helped them expand to stores in the surrounding neighborhood and how we would execute street sampling, in-store demos, point-of-sale displays, public relations, events, social media, and other strategies to educate the right consumers. I explained how the yoga students were drinking Zico as a post-workout recovery drink and loved the fact that it was all natural and high in electrolytes. They were our core audience and the type of customer who loved to tell people about new products they believed in. They were becoming ambassadors for the Zico brand. "Okay," said Lewis, "that's great, but how many yoga studios are there?"

I said New York had about a dozen Bikram studios, maybe fifty including other types of hot yoga. But yoga was more than the people who practiced it every day. It was now a lifestyle. Lululemon was building a billion-dollar brand riding this cultural trend. Yoga was also just the tip of the iceberg. This past summer, I told them, we began to expand distribution to gyms, dance studios, bike shops, as well as natural and gourmet stores. I explained that we had reached out to nutritionists, high-end personal trainers, yoga instructors, and spinning instructors, and they were talking about Zico to their audiences. That we were expanding our marketing to endurance athletes and reaching them at running, cycling, and triathlon events.

"For once, someone listened to me! That's impressive. I like it," said Lewis.

"Consumers aren't just more knowledgeable about ingredients, they are increasingly becoming attuned to the information that their bodies are sending them," I said. "Exercise these days isn't just about making your body look better; it's about *feeling* better both in your body and mind. That's what's drawing people to yoga and it's also why people are moving toward natural, no-sugar-added, and lower-calorie drinks like Zico. People aren't just drinking Zico; they are experiencing the impact on their bodies and they are getting pretty excited about the results. This goes way beyond yoga. There is a much broader audience that is ready for this trend."

"So where do you go from here?" Lewis asked. "Who's funding this operation anyway and how big is your team?"

"Our full-time team is three," I said, "which includes me. We have six demo people we bring on occasionally, nine if you include Maura and our girls, who do events regularly. We're on pace to hit a million dollars in sales this year and we're ready to step on the gas but need to raise more money."

"You're definitely going to need a lot more money and a real team. And you better move fast, those Vita Coco guys are really aggressive. Why haven't you come to us for help sooner?" Before I could answer, Lewis continued, "Come back to us in a couple weeks with a plan for 2008. No pie-in-the-sky bullshit about cultural trends. Spell out how much money you'll need, who you'll hire, what accounts we should go after, what marketing support you'll give us, and all that crap. Work with Dan first and then Jerry and then bring it to me. If it looks right, Big Geyser might invest and I'd highly recommend you give a chance for some of our senior team to do so personally as well. No one wants to miss the boat on the next Vitaminwater, but you've got to convince us you are in that league."

CHAPTER 8
RUNNING THROUGH WALLS

Over the holidays in 2007, I was putting the finishing touches on a plan to take us from $1 million in sales that year to $4 million in 2008. Given Big Geyser's renewed interest in the brand, I believed most of that growth could come from New York itself and that we could take our monthly case volume from four thousand to twelve thousand in that city alone. To do so I believed we'd need a team of at least four: a manager and two area sales managers (ASMs) in addition to Chris plus a field marketing manager to run events, demos, and guerrilla marketing. We would hire a crew of interns to ramp up our coverage during the summer, rehire a public relations firm, and buy or lease a couple of vehicles for street demos and events. We'd hire one more person to help Ross, a young United States Naval Academy grad I had hired to handle all the back office operations.

The plan for 2008 was not only about New York. It included continuing to expand into Whole Foods and other natural food stores, online through Amazon, direct to yoga studios across the country, and to launch in a few to-be-determined markets later in the year. But most of the resources would be focused on New York. To fund all of those expenses and meet that goal, I estimated we'd need to raise $1.5 million.

I walked through the plan with Dan Reade from Big Geyser, who helped me refine it, and then I brought it to Jerry Reda. Jerry listened, asked some questions, and finished by saying, "You need more people. Three ASMs is just not enough." I responded, "I think this is the right number to start with and we'll build from there. Don't forget we've included at least six summer interns and we may be able to flex that up." Lewis echoed Jerry's concern that we needed more people, but in the end agreed we had a working plan.

Big Geyser as a company, plus Lewis, Jerry, Dan, Steven, and a few other executives individually, committed to invest in the new round if we were able to raise the full $1.5 million. Smart investors know their money may be worthless if the company is not fully capitalized, so they often make their commitments contingent on you hitting the entire amount you want to raise. My advisers Jim Tonkin and Jack Belsito both committed to invest and agreed to serve on our board of advisers (which would later morph into a board of directors), along with Lewis from Big Geyser and friend and investor Peter Brodsky. Those investments also signaled a huge vote of confidence that industry insiders thought Zico was going to break through. Better yet, I didn't even have to brag about the investments because in the incestuous beverage industry, word traveled fast.

By mid-January I had commitments for $1.8 million from a total of thirty new investors and for the first time was in the fortunate position of deciding to take more money than planned or turn people away. We took more because I believed it was smart to raise money when I could, even if it meant taking slightly more dilution to our ownership stake. A little extra cash when used well (or conserved) can go a long way to ensuring you stay in business and deliver growth.

And I had been through almost running out of money enough times now to know you always need more. Investors came in between $25,000 and $250,000, with an average of about $50,000. Typically, taking anything less than $25,000 is more hassle than it's worth and I suggest entrepreneurs set a minimum of $50,000 or even $100,000 from any investor and make exceptions only rarely for highly value-added individuals. Among the new investors were industry vets: Tom Scott and Tom First, founders of Nantucket Nectars; Seth Goldman, founder of Honest Tea; and a number of current or past executives from Vitaminwater, Fuze, and Muscle Milk, all of whom had seen the growth of Zico at Big Geyser firsthand. The owners of Bikram Yoga NYC studios in New York and Funky Door Yoga in Berkeley, California, knew how well Zico sold in their studios and excitedly invested as well.

What made this run of good luck more remarkable was that it was happening in the early months of 2008, the same time period that the world economy had basically gone off a cliff. Although financial markets were in terrible shape and liquidity had completely dried up for many businesses, I was able to raise $1.8 million in sixty days when I had spent the last three years raising less than $500,000. What changed?

First of all, I now had a real story to tell investors. Zico wasn't just a pipe dream anymore. We had data, information, and a track record we could point to as evidence of traction. Second, I was targeting industry insiders for funding: people who knew the business and could see what was happening and understand the potential of Zico. Third, we had momentum on our side. With commitments from Big Geyser and a few other early investors to get the ball rolling, I was able to speak to people and not hard sell: I shared the facts and was giving them an opportunity to invest alongside other knowledgeable investors. Finally, I had regained my own confidence. I had been humbled and a little beaten down by the business over the previous years, but now my demeanor showed I was going to do what it took to get through any challenges we would face. I found that smart investors appreciated that I was battle worn and realistic about the likely risks.

TEAM CAPTAIN

At the same time invested capital started coming into the business, I was figuring out how to build out our team. I knew the next hire was critical and I wanted to make sure it was someone who could lead our efforts in New York. With Coke's purchase of Vitaminwater, I assumed some of their employees would be looking to leave. Most of the ones I knew did not strike me as the Coke corporate types, so I figured they'd be looking for their next adventure. I had my eye on one guy in particular: Andrew Griffiths. At the time, Andrew, or Andy as he went by, was responsible for all of Vitaminwater and Smartwater's sales in Manhattan and a few boroughs. He managed a team of at least ten, almost triple that including summer interns and blitz events. He was a strapping, good-looking guy in his early thirties, a constant jokester. When he walked through Big Geyser's warehouse it was fist bumps, high fives, and verbal sparring all around. Zico definitely needed some of his streetwise mojo. Well if you can't beat 'em, I thought, you can hire 'em. Jerry Reda had hinted to me that Andy was looking around and I better move fast. I called him and asked him if we could meet the next afternoon near his home in Hoboken, New Jersey.

Because he was a local, I let him pick the place and when I showed up at the designated address, I found it was a hipster bar. I wasn't surprised Andy had picked a bar to meet. He was testing me out. That was fine with me as I was ready for a beer. My day had begun at five a.m. with a visit to Big Geyser, followed by a few hours on the streets, then hours doing bills, forecasting next production needs, and staying up to date on e-mail. I found Andy already at the bar. He was wearing jeans, flip-flops, and a T-shirt that showed off the tattoos on his biceps.

We both ordered a beer (local craft IPAs of course). We didn't talk about the job at first but had a more general conversation about our lives. I told him about my family and he talked about his girlfriend, Dana, and his passion for the outdoors, particularly kayaking and snowboarding.

"What's your dream?" I asked. "Where do you want to end up?"

He told me that in the short run he wanted to work for a brand he could be excited about, help scale, and have some fun with. He expected a decent salary with a piece of the upside if things really took off. He didn't want to be VP of sales—too much stress and pressure.

"And in five years," he said, "honestly I want to be where the snow is softer, the rivers are faster, and the waves are bigger."

He told me he loved Zico and that he regularly swapped with Chris Michaels, my sole sales rep, two cases of Vitaminwater for one of Zico. He said I shouldn't give Chris a hard time, it's just how the business works and that all the different brands at Big Geyser watch out for each other on the streets. He said, "A lot of our reps love Zico, and I assume you know half your consumers are drinking it as a hangover cure. How the hell did you come up with the idea to start a coconut water business?" I told him my story starting with my time in the Peace Corps and about making an impact on people's health, creating good jobs in tropical countries, and creating a great place to work. It all seemed to resonate with him.

I also learned some insider stories about his years at Vitaminwater. For Andy, it had been a fun and fast ride for sure but he felt something was missing. The company's culture pushed the limits of excess and even decadence. Their weekly office parties often turned into all-nighters, which sometimes included hiring strippers. On one particularly rowdy occasion someone hired a midget-tossing team. Office affairs and one-nighters seemed to be the norm. All of this might have damaged morale in the long run but it appeared there was never a planned long run with Vitaminwater. The company was built to flip: grow fast at all costs and then sell. But Andy seemed most disappointed in the product itself, which he thought only had the pretense of being healthy. In fact, he told me, the staff often referred to it among themselves as "dirty water."

"I don't drink the stuff anymore," Andy admitted, "and I'm no prude when it comes to people having fun. But I'm ready for something different. I'd like to promote a product I believe in and work in a culture that's got a little more, I guess, soul." He said that even if Vitaminwater had not sold to Coke, he would probably be looking to leave. But now with Coke involved he definitely did not want to stay. "I graduated from Frostburg State and it took five years," Andy said with a smile. "The buttoned-down Coke execs of the world don't get guys like me, and the feeling is mutual."

"Do you think it's possible," I said, "to create the same fun, focused, run-through-walls culture you had at Vitaminwater but give it some soul? Have that sort of passion but with a purpose?"

Andy smiled and thought for a moment. "I don't see any reason why we shouldn't give it a try," he said, and we toasted the idea with our pints.

"Okay," I said, "I need to work on the details, but conceptually here's the deal: I'll bring you on as head of northeast sales. You hire and train a great team for New York. Get all the Big Geyser route owners on our side and once you triple our sales and hire and train your replacement, I'll do everything I can to get you out west where you can find those higher mountains and bigger waves."

He answered, "I like the sound of that and so will Dana." We shook hands and within two weeks, we had ironed out the details and Andy was on board.

Most interviews I had over the course of Zico went this way. They were much more about open discussions, alignment of values, and recruiting people for a mission, not just hiring them for a job. In order to make sure hires would thrive in our culture, I communicated openly about our vision and plan. Equally important was that I discovered what each of my potential hires wanted out of life and how I could help them achieve those goals. What were their passions, dreams, and motivations? I wasn't looking for answers I'd predetermined in advance nor did I expect perfect alignment with my own goals and interests. Rather, if I could honestly offer them a path to achieve their life goals, I knew they were more likely to do whatever it took for Zico to be successful.

PASSION, OWNERSHIP, AND A SENSE OF URGENCY

As I was beginning to build an actual team in the spring of 2008, the buzz in the business world was about how to create vibrant and healthy "organizational cultures." "After working on strategy for twenty years, I can say this: culture will trump strategy, every time," strategist Nilofer Merchant wrote in the *Harvard Business Review*. "If the strategy conflicts with how a group of people already believe, behave, or make decisions it will fail." *Forbes* had named organizational culture the "hottest topic in business today." *Entrepreneur* magazine said cultivating a company culture that attracts top talent was one of five best practices the top 10 percent of U.S. companies have in common.

The culture of an organization starts with the founder but grows and changes organically with each hire. Every hire matters. The impact of a new personality coming on board is heightened for small companies who don't have the luxury or ability to address anything in silos. Everything is interconnected and every new employee will likely have an impact on all facets of your business—including the overall culture of the workplace.

Zappos knows that having "employee fit" is so important they offer $2,000 to trainees to leave at the end of training if they don't feel it is the right company or position for them. In their first days and weeks, after they've had a chance to experience the culture, Zappos encourages them, literally pays them, to leave. Zappos knows $2,000 is a small price to pay in order to avoid keeping the wrong hire in their organization.

The corporate world has a wonderful philosophy about hiring great talent wherever and whenever you find it, even creating roles for the right candidate or building what people call "bench strength." I myself used this with great success at International Paper and even at the latest stages of Zico, but in the early, lean years, unless you have funding to cover two or three years of operations, this approach just isn't feasible.

For early stage, modestly funded companies, my advice is, hire when it hurts. When you or your team can't possibly work more hours. When you're stretched to your limit. When it's painfully clear to you, your organization, your customers, partners, or others that you just need more help. That's the time to hire.

That being said, you should always look out for great talent, cultivating relationships and getting to know potential hires in your industry. This strategy allows for more effective just-in-time hiring so you have the bench strength on reserve to hire when it hurts but aren't paying for anyone to sit on the sidelines. For example, I had known and worked for three years with Chris Weavers in Thailand before we brought him in to be Zico's VP of operations. That we knew each other and he knew our organization allowed him to step in and immediately begin to add value. While you won't be able to do this for every hire, hiring when it hurts has two added benefits: it will give your team an opportunity to stretch until that next role is filled, and it lessens the possibility that if you need to scale back, you can while avoiding layoffs.

Hire Bottom Up

Some entrepreneurs attempt to build out the perfect team of experienced senior executives out of the gate. There's some strong evidence to support what Jim Collins calls getting the right people on the bus and letting them determine the direction. But I did not take this approach at Zico. After letting go of the early team I had, I started rebuilding the team carefully. I wasn't looking for people who would look good in a boardroom or had fancy degrees from top schools, but rather street hustlers and hands-on doers. I favored young, aggressive, energetic types, willing to do whatever it took from packing out store shelves to packing boxes.

TOMS Shoes built their company on this sort of energy. In their first year of operation in 2006, Blake Mycoskie and his team of three interns had sold ten thousand shoes out of his small apartment in Venice Beach. A few years later he would build out a senior executive team but most of them came from early hires who were doers, not managers, and they still run one of the best internship programs around.

When it comes to more senior hires, the best are the ones who have had enough corporate experience to know what your business can look like at scale but have also been through a start-up experience to help navigate through all the challenges of smaller stages. Don't be their first fling. Let them learn about start-ups somewhere else and bring that experience to you.

Build a Superteam, Not a Team of Superstars

For generations, the superstar performers have been thought essential to building a great organization. "People say the most important thing is building a world-class team," Ben Horowitz wrote in his book *The Hard Thing about Hard Things*. "It's such an obvious statement to the point where it's useless. It gives you overconfidence if you're doing it because you think that once you have great people, it'll work. But no, it's not that simple. They might end up killing each other if you don't put them together the right way, if you don't make sure people are communicating and on the same page."

I believe that for most businesses, having a superteam rather than a few superstars is far better. Superstars don't come without cost. For a start-up running mean and lean, you might simply not have the cash to lure one of these players or keep them if you're lucky enough to attract them. And in truth, they can embody the very opposite of what makes a good team member. They can be egotists, obsessed only with their own performance. They can make your workplace toxic by becoming competitive with other employees and dismissive of their effort and contribution.

"For the last fifty years, we've thought that success is achieved by picking the superstars," says serial business founder and author Margaret Heffernan in her 2015 TED Women talk. "Pick the brightest men or women and give them all the resources and all the power. But this often leads only to aggression, dysfunction, and waste."

There may be problems in the world that require super-geniuses to solve, but how to effectively promote, market, and sell coconut water wasn't one of them. What I needed were not brilliant individuals but a group with collective intelligence and grit. Self-motivation, integrity, and fitting into the organization's culture were more important than exceptional individual performance and brute intelligence. We looked for one's ability to live the brand—to represent the mission, the company, me, and everything we stood for, whether on the job or off with friends and family.

I also brought as many people as possible into the decision-making process for each hire. This extra step of course made the process increasingly cumbersome as the staff grew. And while the final decision was still mine, by consulting with as many people as possible, I'm convinced I headed off several bad hires when others noticed personalities or interpersonal styles were going to clash.

Play to Strengths

Early in my career, I embraced a management philosophy and practice called the Performance Development Road Map. As part of this process, each employee takes an in-depth personality test that shows areas of strengths, weaknesses, and opportunities to improve relative to some ideal person in that role. Then, the manager is expected to work with the employee to take on tasks, assignments, or education to strengthen the employee's weak areas. I used this for a few years before realizing it was absolutely the wrong way to manage. I was trying to force everyone to become like some generic ideal employee. Not only will this approach not get the best results, its goal is rarely achievable.

We should play to our own strengths no matter what size organization we work in. Within Zico I took this approach starting with myself, recognizing and playing to my strengths, and then hiring others to complement or fill in the gaps. Generally, I'm best at laying out a vision, developing strategy, planning, inspiring people to share and adopt that vision. But what I found out quickly was this skill set was almost zero help when trying to engage Big Geyser distributors. So I hired Andy, who was a lighthearted, street-smart jokester. He could engage with distributors and buyers while I worried about the thirty-thousand-foot view of the business. One of Andy's first hires was Rory Mulcahy. Rory can talk, if you forced him to, though most people thought of him as constantly angry. This couldn't have been further from the truth. He's just not Mr. Big Personality like Andy, but ask him to build and execute a sales plan for New York and track and measure results? Nobody was better. We needed each one of these three very different skill sets and many more to win.

Empowering employees is every leader's dream. We'd all love to have a team that takes initiative and exceeds goals with little guidance. In my experience that's a pipe dream, especially in the early stage of a company. Managers must manage. At Zico I always tried to make very clear what my expectations were and checked in constantly to ensure they were being achieved, at least at the beginning of a new employee's tenure, or after a change of direction or someone taking a new role. This wasn't simply command and control: I always invited feedback and suggestions but once we agreed on the objectives, I wanted to see people deliver. Then when someone proved they could deliver consistently, I would empower them to take it to another level.

We had hired Katie Journeay to lead our expansion into Texas, beginning in Austin. After spending time in New York to get to know the team and how we built Zico there, Katie headed back to Austin to replicate the strategy. The basic plan was the same: distribution in yoga studios and natural foods stores including Whole Foods, and stage demos and events around yoga and endurance sports events, such as running, cycling, and triathlons. For about eighteen months, Katie followed that to a T and her results were extraordinary. She proved that our strategy could work outside of New York. At some point Katie came to me suggesting a new influencer group. She wanted us to sponsor a local roller derby team. I wasn't buying it.

"Roller derby? Are you serious?" I asked.

"Yeah," she said. "It's hot. Where have you been?"

"I don't know, raising children, starting a company," I responded.

"Trust me," she went on. "It's like coconut water, something old coming back with new vigor for a new generation."

I grilled her at length. Had she fully executed our strategy? How many yoga events and triathlons were there in Austin? How many runs? How many had we been involved in? She rattled off all the stats.

"Mark, there's not a yogi, runner, cyclist, or triathlete within one hundred miles of Austin that doesn't know about Zico. We hit fifteen events in the last sixty days alone. We'll keep hitting them but it's time to expand our audience." She then broke down the demographic of the roller derby enthusiasts and their growing fan base. It was an interesting subculture of trendsetters in Austin.

I agreed. Katie had delivered all that I asked, so why not trust she knows what targets to expand into? I don't think roller derby made the difference in our success, but I know that Katie did. And allowing her to experiment in her market kept her more engaged and *thinking* instead of simply executing. Empowerment is risky but if you have the right team, the right guardrails, the right sense of ownership, there is no more powerful way to engage your team. And the results of a fully engaged team have no limits.

When You Make Hiring Mistakes, Undo Them Quickly

You will make mistakes with hires. I made a few bad ones at Zico, usually when I didn't fully engage my team in the hiring process. One senior executive, for example, came highly recommended, was well qualified on paper, and interviewed great. I hired him quickly to fill an important role. Over the first few weeks I was personally engaged much less than I should have been as I was trying to resolve supply chain issues abroad. After about three weeks I got a call from one of my employees who said, "Mark, we need to talk urgently about Max" (not his real name). I was about to get on a plane and said, "I literally have one minute, get to the point." He paused and said, "Let me put it this way. As a team, we have calls before our scheduled calls with him so we can get each other aligned and be prepared to stand up to him and then we have calls afterward to debrief. It's killing us."

I dug deeper and it appeared this person had somehow managed to alienate much of the company, especially the field sales and marketing organizations, in just a few weeks. I talked to him, laid out the facts. He knew it was true and we both recognized that Zico had a very unique and almost fanatically protective and passionate culture, and he was never going to recover. I took responsibility and we parted ways amicably. With one wrong hire, I could have destroyed everything we had built. Fortunately, our team felt comfortable to come to me and when it was obvious this hire needed to go, the company basically purged him—he didn't belong in the Zico culture. That's not to say that he wouldn't perform well in a different organization. Fit and alignment is key to hiring the right team.

Why Women Reach Higher

When I first immersed myself in the beverage industry, I was stunned to realize how few women were in leadership roles of entrepreneurial companies. The Coca-Cola Company and PepsiCo had numerous women in senior roles, all the way to the top spot at PepsiCo. But among start-ups, I met only a few women in major roles and only one that I recall running the show. The common thinking among some in the industry was that the start-up beverage world was so cutthroat and competitive that only ruthless, self-absorbed jerks stood a chance. That myth selects for men. (Name all the ruthless, self-absorbed jerks you've met and see how many women end up on your list.) For those who don't believe that myth and build their businesses on entirely different values, you have a huge competitive advantage to be gained in the wellspring of talent that is not being considered.

When I hired women for senior roles in finance, operations, sales, and marketing, I heard whispers from some in the industry that they weren't going to be tough enough. Those spreading rumors clearly didn't know these women. Their form of toughness didn't come from mirroring the testosterone-fueled behavior of men but from a brutal assessment of the facts and a hard-nosed and honest take on what needed to happen for the best of the business, and they kept me in line on more than one occasion.

Indeed, if honesty and adherence to ethical behavior is central to your corporate culture, women should be at the top of your list. After the Enron scandal, researchers from Penn State using the federal government's Corporate Fraud Task Force found that only 9 percent of the 436 defendants in federal corporate fraud cases between 2002 and 2009 were women and only three of those were women identified as "ringleaders." Of those three, only one was not married to another ringleader. And in the top ten worst accounting scandals in history, all leading players were men. I'm not going to attempt to explain this other than to say it doesn't surprise me in the least.

Your business is unlikely to experience corporate fraud but I believe these statistics speak to a larger truth. Ethical behavior is not just about the big moments that break laws but hundreds of small decisions that occur every day. In my experience, women are more likely than men to prioritize those small displays of integrity: coming through on promises, not cutting corners, and showing respect for all parties. That behavior tends to set the tone for everyone around her.

I'm not the only one to realize the value of this untapped potential, and the climate for women is changing quickly. I've been blown away by the millennial female entrepreneurs I've met in the last few years across all industries. They are wicked smart, incredibly competent, driven, and competitive. But most also appear to have their egos under control, have a bigger sense of the world and their companies' role in it. They not only are out to make a buck but also lead with caring and compassion. Many of them have been an inspiration to me and helped me understand and become excited about what the future holds.

WHEN IT ALL COMES TOGETHER

Organizational culture gets established quickly. Shortly after joining in January of 2008, Andy had built a small but passionate and effective sales team that included Chris, Rory, Drew, Carolina, and Carol. Shortly after, we added Ryan in sales and James to focus on marketing. Ross and Sherif handled operations and managed the direct sales to yoga studios out of my garage. They all lived and breathed the Zico brand. The field team started their days at six a.m. at Big Geyser, sucking on diesel fumes. Their way of breaking through with route owners was straightforward. Bring a dozen bagels, a box of donuts, and some coffee. Their goal was to get the attention of every route owner and learn what made each of them tick. Then after you have their attention, the work begins to gain their trust.

Earning trust with the route guys was not easy. These route owners spent years building relationships with some of the toughest store owners and managers in New York City, and they weren't about to allow anyone to walk in and screw it all up. When the Friday whistle blew, Andy's team woke up the next morning to pass out cartons of Zico at weekend running or triathlon events across the New York metro area. In order to gain the distributors' trust, they would need to do whatever it took to get and keep Zico on retailers' shelves, as well as make sure it sold off.

For example, they knew that they had to make sure Zico was perfectly merchandized. All the other beverage brands were fighting for the same precious space in the cooler; that perfect, eye-to-thigh spot near the front of the store. To get it, the Zico team had to want it more. If that meant helping distributors build displays at three a.m. at a Whole Foods Market, then that is what they did. They performed their own demos, staffed their own events, put up point-of-sale displays, and talked to everyone and anyone about Zico.

I was awed by what they accomplished. I had read for years about the concept of high-performing teams and had helped mold some during my corporate days, but here I had the good fortune to see what could happen when a team formed and developed right before my eyes. There would be a constant chatter of texts and e-mails with photos and updates: "Just opened a hip coffee shop in Brooklyn, check out this display" or "Another 100-case order for Fairway," always with pictures attached. Or when they needed help, "Ross, please take the van to Westside Market on 45th. Need to drop 20 cases and a rack. I'll be there at 3:30. Can anyone help me build an 80-case display?"

You also had to stay on your toes with this team, as they were pranksters. They told me that the owner of a new yoga account was excited to meet me and that I should get there at precisely three thirty p.m. on any weekday. I did and discovered I'd just walked into the middle of the all-male class at Hot Naked Yoga NYC. This level of constant communication (and practical jokes) would be the mode of operation for our sales and marketing field teams as they grew from this small New York group to cover a dozen major cities across the country. And they coined a term for that communication: "cowbell," referring to the *Saturday Night Live* skit where Christopher Walken's character demands that band member Will Ferrell give "more cowbell." I liked to think I was Walken but maybe they thought of me as a backup singer. I never asked.

I got a clear picture of how strong and effective our company culture had become one day in the summer of 2008, when I went to Big Geyser to drop in on my team's daily sales meeting. Before I went into the main offices, I walked around the warehouse to get a look at the first ever delivery truck we'd wrapped with the Zico brand. Most of the one-hundred-plus vehicles in Big Geyser's fleet were decorated (or "wrapped" as they say in the business) with the design of one of the beverage brands the company carried. It cost three or four thousand dollars (plus a few hundred thrown in to cover small repairs the driver wanted done while the truck was off the road) to make these driving billboards. Vitaminwater or Smartwater covered probably 40 percent of the Big Geyser fleet. Negotiating to get one on J Bev's route on the West Side of Manhattan was a small coup by Andy and the team, and I was excited to see the truck roll out the doors in the early morning light. I wondered how many thousands of people that day might glance at the truck's panels as it made its way around Manhattan, especially the big Zico package on the truck's roof.

The truck wasn't the only sign that Zico had moved up in status from an interesting little brand to a company that was getting real attention. While I once felt like an outsider in the Big Geyser warehouse, it now felt like a second home, and I was treated like family by everyone from the executives to the administrative staff. The drivers, who were now making some meaningful money with Zico, would at least say hello and wanted to shake my hand.

That morning I found my team in the conference room usually reserved for only Big Geyser staff meetings, with six of our salespeople and one from marketing at the table. Andy, who was in charge, started the meeting with little preamble. "I hope everyone saw the new truck," he said. "We've been called up to the big leagues. Time to show 'em we deserve to be here."

What followed was a rapid-fire status check from everyone in the room.

"Ryan," he started, "what's the status of Fairway?"

"They ordered a pallet load per store, which arrived on Monday. I went to both stores yesterday and they're blowing through it, so I don't think it's going to get them through the weekend."

"Can you get Antonio to put in another order today?" Andy asked.

"Did it last night," Ryan said with a smile. "It's on that big blue truck that just went out the door."

"Son of a bitch, you stole my thunder," Andy said. "Enough with you. Chris, tell me some good news about Whole Foods in Chelsea?"

When the sales team was done, James ran down a list of the ten upcoming events from a triathlon in the Hamptons to a yoga competition in Manhattan.

"Wait," interrupted one of the sales reps. "Did you say yoga competition? Do you win by sitting still the longest?"

"Of course not," James said deadpan and without missing a beat. "It's Bikram. It's the guy who sweats the most. Actually, it's going to be a great event for Zico, and Mark, I may have told the organizers that you were coming."

"Already planning on it. I'm bringing Maura and the girls," I said. "But I'm not competing. I'm too good, it wouldn't be fair."

James then handed out packets of the recent online and mainstream media hits from the previous month. It was a thick stack, and James was clearly pleased with the thump each packet made as it hit the table. Zico had been mentioned or pictured in *Men's Fitness, Luxury Hotelier, Curve, In Touch Weekly, Star Magazine*, and more. He also reported that Gwyneth Paltrow, Liv Tyler, and Robert De Niro had all either mentioned drinking Zico or had been photographed with a carton in their hands.

"Nice!" Andy jumped in. "Make sure to tell De Niro that Gwyneth and I will take a complimentary table at his new restaurant next week but please make it a good one. Gwyn hates when we're stuck near the kitchen."

James said, "I almost forgot, I just got pinged this morning that Rachael Ray does this segment called 'What's in Your Fridge.' They featured this model Jacqueline and when she opened her fridge she had celery sticks and like six Zicos!"

As we were about to finish up, Carl Gaglio, Big Geyser operations manager, poked his head in the room.

"Hey, look at this, you even invited Mark to the party! Hey guys, sorry to interrupt, but Mark, I'm glad you're here. I just got another two-hundred-case order from FreshDirect and another big order just went out to Fairway. I'm not sure what the hell you guys are doing but I don't think I have enough product to get through the week and just want to see if we can get a rush order of a couple pallets by tomorrow morning."

"We've got you covered," I said. "How much are you thinking?"

"Full truck load, Carl!" Andy jumped in. "Look at this team. We're just getting warmed up and you've got to be ready."

It was a great bit of public arm-twisting by Andy. Big Geyser liked to order pallet loads at a time, even multiple times per week to keep their inventory as low as possible. The fact that they might be up to a full truck of five thousand cases for next-day delivery was a big deal. Everyone looked to Carl in anticipation.

"Full truck load it is," he said, smiling at the hoots and hollers from the group.

What pumped me up wasn't just that Zico was selling well but that this team was working like a well-oiled machine. And they were having fun, too. There was barely a beat between Andy's rapid-fire questions and clear, concise, knowledgeable answers. When problems or issues came up, no time was wasted pointing fingers or avoiding blame. Everyone's focus was on the solution. I jumped in once or twice, making a few suggestions, but for the most part, I stood on the sidelines, a proud coach watching his team execute play after play and thinking, "If we can replicate this in every major market in the country, someday Zico will be huge."

As the summer of 2008 came to a close, we decided to run an incentive with the route owners for September and October. The overall goal was to show them and the Big Geyser team that Zico could scale, and we were willing to pay a price to prove that point. With Big

Geyser's help, we structured the so-called Battle of the Boroughs to make it enticing but fair by handicapping boroughs against each other. For each territory we were offering five-hundred-dollar cash prizes for each route owner that could sell the most volume and another five hundred dollars to the person who increased his percentage the most over the prior year's sales.

We had their attention and focus, and to make sure the distributors were successful, we executed a weeklong blitz at the beginning and the end of the contest. During those weeks our entire team of eleven, including recently hired Michael "Buck" Williams and Rory Mulcahy in New York, Carlos and Juliet, who had recently been hired in Los Angeles, a few interns, and me, worked with distributors in each territory to help them sell more cases. Every day our team would meet at Big Geyser at five a.m. Rory had masterminded a detailed schedule of who worked with which distributor in which territory, matching personalities, considering every detail. We had a list of target accounts, goals for the day for new accounts and cases sold, and two vans circling the city with cases, racks, point of sale, T-shirts, hats, and coolers. When not dropping off product or racks to support the sales effort, this team hit select spots for guerrilla street demos like Union Square or the Columbus Circle entrance of Central Park or in front of Vita Coco's offices (just for the hell of it), always avoiding (or sampling) the police as we had none of the required permits to do these street demos.

At the end of October we were scheduled to present the awards at the monthly Big Geyser sales meeting. Just the year before, we were rarely if ever on the monthly schedule; this time we were the main event. Our whole team was waiting outside as the Vitaminwater team funneled out. Since the Coke purchase they had lost some of their mojo. Many on their team had been recruited away to other brands and Coke wasn't hiring replacements, so our team began to rival theirs in size, energy, and passion. Someone opened the door and called, "Zico!" and we all plowed into the room—the energy was palpable.

Though I was there, Andy took the lead. This was his show. He knew how hard the route owners had worked, and that you don't take credit for what just happened; you give them all the credit. "Guys, we really appreciate the phenomenal work these past two months. Big Geyser broke twelve thousand cases this month, three times last year's volume." Our team started cheering and the room followed along. Andy continued. "That's incredible and I hope you can now all see the power of the Zico brand. I also want to personally thank you because Mark made me a promise that if I tripled the New York business, built the right team, and found my replacement, he'd move me to L.A. to do the same out there. So I'm out of here soon. Thanks to you we tripled the business! You can see, and I think all know now, we have a great team, and while no one could ever replace me, I found this guy, Buck Williams, out on the street looking for work. Let us get to the fun stuff now and tell you what you really want to hear: who won the incentives for the month. Buck, take it away. Buck Williams, everybody."

Everyone cheered and some yelled profanities. They knew and loved Buck. He had been at Vitaminwater for several years and recently took over as Zico manager for all of New York. With two of Vitaminwater's best people on Zico's team, they knew we were serious.

Buck went to the front. "Thank you, Andy, I think. I've only been working with Zico officially for a week and I could go on but enough about me and certainly enough about Andy, let's give away some cash money!" Everyone screamed at this.

"So here are the results! Andy, drumroll, please!" Keeping a showman's pace, Andy gave out the prizes. The five hundred dollars cash was no huge deal to these guys but Andy's presentation, which was equal parts praise and not-so-gentle ribbing, made it feel like a real event. One by one, route owners from various New York areas came up to get their reward.

Andy saved Joey Bev, who covered Harlem, for last. In a month, Joey had quintupled his sales of Zico from 72 to 360 cases. Joey, all 225 pounds of solid muscle, barreled his way to the front of the room to get his cash, but Andy pulled away the envelope at the last moment and handed it to Buck.

"Not so fast, remember," Buck said. "Some of you may have heard that we had a little side bet going on, right, Joey? Although fifteen years past his prime, Joey still considers himself somewhat of an athlete having played tailback in a semipro football league in Finland or somewhere and thinks he can take me in a fifty-yard dash."

Only Buck, who knew Joey well, could get away with this next comment. "What he calls muscle, I'm calling flab! So guess what we're going to do? Joey, I'm gonna race ya! Right here, right now, out on the mean streets of Maspeth. Trucks, exhaust, and potholes be damned! Double or nothing."

The distributors and Big Geyser team loved it. All the route owners were cheering and hollering and placing side bets with each other. In that moment I could tell, mostly thanks to Andy and Buck, Zico had become accepted into the rough-and-tumble Big Geyser family. The incentives we could offer as a small brand were also small, but our energy and ability to make it fun for these hardworking route owners made a big difference.

Everyone poured out onto the street and someone marked off a start and finish to fifty yards. Another person offered to get their Glock for an official start but was talked out of it by others. Buck and Joey lined up; Andy stood in front and set them off. Joey was unbelievably quick for a big guy and took off like a cheetah and to everyone's surprise Buck, who still is a great athlete himself, never caught up, or he never tried. Everyone cheered.

After Joey cooled down, I walked up to him with the original envelope with five hundred dollars and peeled off five more hundreds to go on top and said congratulations. He took the envelope but wouldn't take the other five hundred dollars. "I earned that, this race, this was for fun. I don't want your money. I told you before not to count out Harlem. They're ready for Zico. Get your team to spend more time with me in my market and you won't regret it, Mark. That's what I want!"

The chaos cleared, traffic resumed, and we gathered the Zico team around and Rory assigned tasks for one last day of blitz. Like everyone, I had my assignment, to visit a few key accounts and present a new program we wanted to run with the Bikram Yoga NYC owners. That night we all met at a little Cuban restaurant in Harlem to celebrate. Andy and Buck gave away awards to the team for the weekly blitz: most accounts opened, most cases sold, best point-of-sale display built. The team ate, drank, and celebrated and a few hours later wound up in Koreatown doing karaoke. After my turn on the stage, which seriously underwhelmed everyone, I headed on a train home to let the team party on. They deserved it. It had been an intense but incredibly productive week, and year for that matter.

We were on track to finish 2008 strong, at $4 million in revenue versus $1 million the year before, but the fight was just beginning. While we were winning battles in New York, the coconut water wars were erupting on multiple fronts across the country and would soon spill into Europe. Although we were perhaps leading Vita Coco in New York, they had a leg up on us in other parts of the country and had recently raised a formidable $10 million to drive growth in

Boston, Los Angeles, and other markets we'd soon learn about. It was time to raise more money and start thinking about an aggressive expansion plan. No better time exists to raise another round of investment than when the final checks of the previous raise have barely cleared your bank account.

CHAPTER 9
DANCING WITH ELEPHANTS

RECESSION-ERA CAPITAL

As fall 2008 was coming to a close, Zico had strong momentum. Not only did we have $4 million in sales projected, but also Zico had become Big Geyser's fastest-growing brand. We had built a strong team in New York, and a two-person team to cover natural food stores like Whole Foods and work with our new broker, Presence Marketing. We were in the process of building a sales and marketing team in Los Angeles and we had signed Haralambos, the top craft beer and non-alcoholic beverage distributor on the West Coast, even though they were already distributing Vita Coco.

The coconut water category was starting to get the attention of the investment world as well. In 2007 Vita Coco had added to their war chest with a $2 million investment from a leading venture capital firm, Verlinvest, with a follow-on investment the next year rumored to be over $10 million. A strong third competitor had also emerged, ONE coconut water, with mainly West Coast distribution. We undoubtedly needed some serious capital to stay in the game. We were able to raise a few million more from our existing investors to fund 2008, but I knew we needed more. We had to raise at least $10 million, and ideally $15 million. That wouldn't happen just passing the hat to friends and family (again), beverage industry executives who could spare $50,000, and a few individual angel investors I knew who had pockets that deep. Now was the time to talk to the professionals. In normal times, given our growth and that of the category, we should not have had a problem convincing a venture capital firm that Zico was a sound investment with a potentially huge upside. We were, at the time, competing to be the number one or number two brand in a new beverage category that was doubling, sometimes tripling, in volume year over year. That sort of scenario doesn't come along very often.

But the financial markets of 2008 were no normal time.

By September 2008, average U.S. home prices had fallen by over 20 percent versus their peak in 2006. Fifteen percent of homes were worth less than the mortgages on them, a number that would climb to 23 percent over the coming years. Although this was certainly only the tip of the iceberg in terms of the underlying financial crisis, when consumers realized they had less wealth in their homes, they stopped spending money on stuff (including investing in stocks), and the U.S. equity markets took a tumble. The Dow Jones Industrial Average, which had peaked at a record high of 14,000 in October 2007, would fall to below 8,000 by December 2008. Economists believed the crisis, which was now global, would cost the U.S. economy alone $22 trillion according to a U.S. Government Accountability Office study.

I was trying to raise $15 million during the worst financial crisis since the Great Depression. So I talked through our options with my adviser Jim Tonkin. He agreed we needed to raise a large amount of capital and I asked him what he thought our chances were of doing so anytime soon. "Look, the long-term outlook for Zico is great," he said.

"People are not going to stop drinking beverages. If anything they become a relatively affordable luxury in tight times. There's plenty of money sitting in these venture firms. They're going to be more cautious and perhaps tougher with their terms but they need to invest somewhere."

I asked him where we should start. "Are you ready to make a pitch next week?" Sure, I said, where? "Let me see if I can get you into NCN. The presenting company list is set, but I'll bet I can get them to squeeze you in."

PITCH PERFECT

So in November of 2008, I flew to San Francisco to speak to a select group of investors at a one-day conference called the Nutrition Capital Network (NCN). That Jim could get me on the bill on such short notice is a testament to the respect he had in the industry. Hundreds of food and beverage companies in the general health, wellness, and nutrition categories apply to present but only a couple of dozen get the nod.

All of the selected companies would present to about thirty-five leading venture capital, private equity, and strategic (meaning corporate) investors. The strategics included Nestlé, Campbell Soup, Kraft, General Mills, and Mars. Lots of other important people were there, including Coke and Pepsi and a who's who of natural food investors.

Generally these investors were looking for companies that had some unique innovation and a chance to break out from the competition and go on to generate at least $100 million in revenue in a reasonable number of years. They all, of course, hoped to spot and invest in the next billion-dollar brand. This wasn't where entrepreneurs came to pitch pie-in-the-sky ideas. With rare exceptions, the companies that presented were already generating between $1 million and $10 million in annual revenue. What they all had in common was that the experienced team at NCN felt there was something special enough about each company that their members/investors would find interesting.

Each company had ten minutes to make their pitch onstage in front of the room of maybe 150 people. In the afternoon was a sort of speed dating process where companies would sit at their designated table while every ten minutes a bell rang and investors would move from one table to the next.

I was scheduled to present late in the morning, and Jim and I met to strategize at breakfast that morning about what would make Zico stand out from the crowd. "What if," I asked Jim, "I went up and told them that I didn't need any money?"

"You're going to tell a group of investors that you don't want their investment?"

"Right," I said. "Everyone is too desperate in this economic climate. I'm going to play hard to get."

"All right," he said. "At least it should get their attention."

I took the stage at my designated time and started off saying that I hoped the organizers wouldn't give me the hook for saying this, but we don't need any capital right now. We just completed another angel financing round, I went on, that would allow us to double our revenues over the next year. Once we've done that, and refined our strategy, we'll know we are truly onto something, then we will need more money to fully capitalize on the opportunity. "So I'd like to introduce you to Zico if you're not familiar with it, explain what we're doing to build the next billion-dollar beverage brand and the positive impact we can make on the world while doing so. I look forward to meeting with some of you afterward if you want to learn more."

I explained what coconut water is and why it was becoming popular. I talked through our New York strategy, our results with Big

Geyser, and how we would replicate it in other markets, following the yogis. I finished by saying, "Not only are we building what we believe will be a great new beverage brand, we're building a whole new category. And the wonderful thing about a coconut water category is first, it's about simple, healthy, natural replenishment. That's something consumers want and the beverage industry should deliver. But additionally, we can help create massive and sustainable economic impact in the tropical world. There are no losers in this scenario. That's what gets me excited and if it does you, too, I look forward to discussing more about it with you this afternoon."

I came down off the stage and the audience broke up for the scheduled coffee break. Jim came up and said, "Nailed it. I took a look at your dance card for the afternoon meetings and it's already full."

When it was time for the speed dating section, I felt like a prince holding court with Jim as my gatekeeper. Nestlé had the first slot and were so excited they blew past their ten minutes and Jim had to interrupt them and say, "Gentlemen, sorry to say your time is up. I'll be back in touch to schedule something in person if you're serious." We met with all the major firms and they all seemed interested.

Over dinner and a nice bottle of wine that night, Jim said, "It's time for a roadshow. The fish are nibbling; let's see if any will bite. But look, nothing's going to happen between now and the New Year so spend some time with Maura and the girls and rest up; 2009 is going to be a wild year."

Jim set up meetings after the New Year to follow up with some of the potential investors we met at NCN. For a few weeks of 2009, we were constantly on the road. One week it was Boston. The next Los Angeles and then up to San Francisco. Late in January we even trekked to Switzerland to meet Nestlé's team.

As long as I was on the road, I figured I'd take the time to learn about other markets. I saw potential for Zico everywhere. In Boston I talked with managers at Whole Foods and met with two potential distributors and visited a few yoga studios. I did the same in San Francisco and spent some time with our early customers at the four Funky Door Yoga studios.

As excited as I was about expanding to these other markets, I knew many a company had failed in the process of expanding from one region of the U.S. to the others. Dunkin' Donuts, an institution in New England since the 1950s, struggled to expand west and had two failed attempts to enter California in the 1990s and again in the early 2000s and only recently figured out the right strategy. You can't necessarily cut and paste what made you successful in one place and assume it will work in the next. I spoke with Steve Fellingham, previous CEO of Carvel ice cream, in the early days of Zico. At its peak Carvel had $300 million in sales per year and had real momentum in the northeast but couldn't find footing in the rest of the country. Steve said, "Be careful. National rollouts are much more expensive and complicated than most people realize."

Those couple of weeks had been a whirlwind, but now I was home in New Jersey spending some time with Maura and the girls and back to running the business while we waited for the term sheets I hoped would start rolling in.

The responses did start coming in but the first few were not encouraging. One firm said they loved the concept and me but the business was just too small. Another said the opportunity was "too binomial: it might work big but might flop completely." Welcome to the beverage business, I muttered under my breath. Another said they were interested, but they were waiting for the financial markets to calm down before they started to invest again. What happened to all the excitement we generated at NCN, I thought.

A week later, Jim called to say that he had spoken to one of the firms and they would be sending a term sheet later that day. "Don't get too excited," he said. "I know these guys and I'm not expecting to be wowed."

I refreshed my e-mail every fifteen minutes or so for the rest of the day and finally saw it come through. The term sheet was attached as a PDF and it was just two pages describing the broad outline of what they were proposing. It seemed simple and straightforward. But as I read the details I was in disbelief. I called Jim. "Do I have this right?" I asked. "They're offering $5 million to own 51 percent of Zico, and if I don't make their target sales figures they'll suddenly own 90 percent?" That meant that my latest investors would effectively lose half of their value since they invested at a valuation of close to $10 million. And that was the best-case scenario. If we didn't achieve the goals they set, effectively every investor would lose 90 percent or more, and Zico would have to become huge to recover that. This is called a "cram down" in the finance world. Basically the new investor squeezes down everyone else's ownership to own more for themselves.

"That's what they seem to be offering," Jim told me. "Look. It's a first offer. Don't freak out, just sleep on it and if it's not right call them and tell them so and let's see how they react. The good news is that having one term sheet on the table makes it easier to get others."

I talked the offer over with Maura as I helped Ciara get ready for bed that night. Ciara was eight at the time and I could see her listening intently. She had lived with the talk of Zico in the background most of her life and had handed out her share of samples at demos and events. We talked about Zico in the family like he was a rambunctious but gifted little brother. Before Maura could jump in with her opinion about the offer, Ciara piped up. "Wait a minute, Daddy," she said in her high-pitched voice that shrouded a mind insightful beyond her years. "You're telling me they will give Zico some money but you don't get to keep any of it yourself and they own half of the company and if you do something wrong they own it all? Why would you do that, Daddy?"

Maura smiled and gave me a nod that said, "I'm going with Ciara on this one."

I called the managing director of that firm the next morning. "Thank you for the term sheet. I talked it over with my eight-year-old daughter and she thought it was a bad deal," I joked, "so I'm going to have to decline.

"Frankly," I went on, "I can't imagine ever being in a situation where I would accept these terms."

"Mark, you do understand that we would figure out a way to make this attractive to you as CEO as you continue to grow the company?"

The underlying message was evident: they would issue more shares to me, as CEO, and perhaps I could earn as much or even more money in the end than if I held on to the ownership I currently had. Unspoken was the likelihood that my earlier investors would take a bath. If properly structured and managed, there is nothing illegal about this and sadly it's not uncommon. If a company is about to go out of business or had been overvalued in an early round, some negative impact to investors may be inevitable. Fortunately, we were not in that situation and I wasn't going to leave my early loyal investors in the dust.

A few weeks later I received a very attractive offer from a VC firm in New York. But it came with a major catch and a strange warning. The firm would put up the entire $15 million investment but only if I somehow managed to get one of the big beverage companies like Coke or Pepsi to sign on as partner. Because of Zico's relatively small size, that would be no small feat. At a meeting where we hammered out the details, one of the partners also called me aside and asked me if I knew a guy named Jesse Itzler. What a strange question, I thought. I told him that I did know Jesse. Well, I knew *of* him. He was one of the guys who had founded Marquis Jet and had become a sort of center of gravity for the celebrity and sports world in New York.

"And you are asking about Jesse because?" I prompted.

"I hear through the grapevine that he's thinking about starting a coconut water brand," he said. "If he does, watch out because he's a monster. Jesse knows everyone. You don't want to go up against him."

Walking away my first reaction was, "Screw this Jesse guy." I was already dealing with some heavy competition. The idea that I should be wary of someone just because he knew some athletes and celebrities was something that I wasn't going to spend my time worrying about.

"Well," Jim said after the meeting, "now all we need is a strategic to throw in a few bucks. Let's start at the top. You take Coke and I'll take Pepsi?"

BRAIN DRAIN

Jim went straight to the top and managed to set up a meeting with PepsiCo's head of mergers and acquisitions. We traveled to their stately headquarters in the rolling hills of Purchase, New York, and drove our cheap rental car past the sculpture garden that included works from Rodin, Calder, Moore, and Giacometti. I couldn't help but think that any one of these pieces of art was probably worth more than Zico at that time. We met the executive alone in a large conference room. He was not a social guy and we had awkward and cold introductions. At the end of my brief presentation I said, "So we have an investor ready to put up all the capital we need, and we'd like to figure out a way for Pepsi to become a minority partner. We don't even want access to your distribution network right away. We think it's too risky for a small brand." The only time he spoke during the whole presentation was to say, "Well, that's surprising, we're very confident in our distribution network's ability to manage and grow small brands." At the end he said, "Thank you for coming. It's all very interesting and we'll get back in touch if we'd like to have any further conversations."

That was it. Walking away, I had the feeling of being drained of information. I also believed he was wrong about the distribution. Putting a young coconut water brand in a funky Tetra Pak package into either Coke's or Pepsi's distribution network right away might be disastrous. I had heard through my Brazilian contacts that PepsiCo was looking into potentially partnering or buying our supplier Amacoco outright, so their standoffishness was understandable. They were potentially looking into cutting off our supply. He didn't see us as future partners—we were future competitors, and he wanted all the details he could gather to win the fight. I was pretty confident that we'd never hear back from PepsiCo again, but I knew sooner or later they would get into the coconut water business.

Everyone in the beverage industry could see that the big players, with Coke being the prime example, were vulnerable with sales of carbonated soft drinks either flat or declining. Speaking in Atlanta in late 2009 to a room full of analysts, investors, and reporters, Muhtar Kent, the CEO of Coca-Cola, admitted that the company had been caught flat-footed by the changing environment.

According to Kent, the company had "not focused enough on the changes taking place with our consumers and customers. In essence, we were too busy looking at the dashboard and were not sufficiently paying attention to the world outside of our windshield." It was an admission that, in not being responsive to cultural currents, they were in danger of running that big red truck off the road and into a ditch.

Carbonated soft drinks, the core of Coke's business, had been in decline on a per capita basis in the U.S. since 1997. In terms of total revenue since 2005, Coke had done a great job fighting for a shrinking pie but that was only going to work for so long. "They missed a lot of trends," was how Bill Pecoriello, CEO of Consumer Edge Research, put it in a 2009 *Ad Age* interview. "There was a shift away from certain beverages and needs being filled by alternative beverages."

To help address this challenge, Coke established a small internal team in 2007 charged with researching and investing in small brands with big potential. "The Venturing and Emerging Brands group was established to try to identify the next big thing," Deryck van Rensburg, the South African–born president and general manager of the group, told an industry reporter. "We see ourselves as intrapreneurs, bridging the gap between big companies and entrepreneurs. Our stated mission is ultimately to develop the next series of brands with billion-dollar potential." And, it went unsaid but understood by all, to buy into those brands long before they had reached the stratospheric valuation of Glacéau.

The Venturing and Emerging Brands team (VEB for short) wasn't placing large numbers of bets on new brands. They considered $10 million in annual revenue to be the "proof of concept" point for the emerging brands they would consider partnering with. That limited their choices greatly, given that only 3 percent of new beverages ever made that cut. Even so, van Rensburg estimated that the VEB team evaluated somewhere between 150 to 200 brands each year. They then eliminated the ones that were too risky or didn't match Coke's long-term consumer vision. With the two dozen or so remaining brands they would then launch a type of soft diplomacy—a series of informal meetings to get to know the entrepreneurs and to "assess the brand's potential and evaluate partnership opportunities." With that information in hand, VEB might offer Coke's investment money and resources for a select two or three brands per year. Despite the word "venturing" in their name, no one in the industry had any illusions that VEB was a venture capital firm that just wanted to make a big return on their investment. They wanted to partner with young brands to help them grow but only if, at the end of the day, Coke could own them outright.

In February of 2008, Coke announced an investment in Honest

Tea. The deal came with an option to buy a majority stake in the future, which Coke would follow through on within three years. From what I could gather, it looked like a smart investment made at the perfect Goldilocks period when Honest Tea was not too big and not too small.

I wasn't the only one impressed by this unusually savvy move on Coke's part. "Coke is working very hard to build up its portfolio of non-carbonated brands," John Sicher, editor of *Beverage Digest*, told *USA Today* in early 2008. "Going back some years, that area of the beverage business was not its strength. Coke is showing that it knows what it needs to do and is doing it."

That VEB also had their eye on Zico was an open secret. They were often visiting the offices of Big Geyser to keep their finger on the pulse of the entrepreneurial beverage community. At the time Big Geyser still distributed Vitaminwater and Smartwater, which were now Coke brands, so the VEB team had a reason to visit. At a Big Geyser monthly sales meeting early in 2008, one of the senior executives at VEB excitedly pulled me aside.

"Mark, you're not going to believe this and I probably shouldn't be telling you this," he said, "but Coke recently spent a ton of money to determine what were the hot trend-setting products. We weren't just looking at beverages. This was food, beverages, and all kinds of lifestyle products. Guess what showed up on the map?"

I pretty much knew where he was going but I didn't want to come off too cocky. "Coconut water?" I offered.

"Not just coconut water," he said excitedly. "Zico, by name! This was a comprehensive study supposed to represent up-and-coming trends across the whole country and little ole Zico made the list. Can you believe it?"

"Actually, I can," I said. "Let me guess: You were focusing on the northeast and particularly on New York because you know that's where a lot of trends are born and influential consumers live. You were also looking for twenty-five- to thirty-five-year-olds, mainly female, who are embracing new cultural trends like yoga or outdoor sports. Basically, you were looking at the very influential audience that we've been targeting and partnering with for the last four years. So yes, I can believe our name made your radar. That was our plan!"

"I can tell you it got people's attention, but as you know Zico is just too small for us to really discuss anything now. Keep doing what you're doing and let's stay in touch."

Coke's interest in Zico formalized a bit when van Rensburg invited me, along with half a dozen beverage entrepreneurs, to a breakfast meeting at Expo West in 2009, an annual food show held in Anaheim, California. VEB had rented a meeting room at the Anaheim Hilton, right across the street from the convention center where the expo was held, and served an elegant and healthy catered breakfast. Included were the founders of Steaz tea, Hint water, Bawls Guarana, and others. Van Rensburg cut the figure of a high-profile executive. With his native South African accent, he was always impeccably dressed and gave off an air of reserve and control. "We think all of you have potential," he told us. "Somewhere in this room is the billion-dollar brand of the future, and Coke would like to help you get there."

At the mention of the word "billion," I could sense the pulse rate of my fellow entrepreneurs go up a bit, but I tried to keep the pitch in perspective. This was little more than an expression of interest and would likely turn into nothing for most or all of the companies in the room. Still, I was pleased that no other coconut water company had been invited to the breakfast. But, for all I knew, the guys from Vita Coco had already heard the same pitch at an earlier time slot.

Given that my offer from the VC firm in New York required that I bring a partner like Coke to the table, I figured it was time to push the question and approach van Rensburg.

I needed to know whether Coke was in or out and I didn't want to burn a year or two waiting to find out. But if I was going to reach out to van Rensburg, I needed to find some way that he could make a personal connection with the Zico brand and ideally me. Everything I knew about him indicated this would be a challenge. He appeared reserved, very professional, polished, and rational, and unlikely swayed emotionally. But I knew one powerful motivator was already at work in the Coke system, and I've found it at work in many of the major consumer products companies these days: fear.

Coke was losing market share and simply couldn't be left out of the next big trend. If Coca-Cola continued to shell out billions of dollars to buy upstart brands, they would likely take a hit on Wall Street for not being a leader in their own industry. What was personal to van Rensburg I'm sure was making this VEB experiment a success, and fear of missing out (FOMO) can be a powerful motivator for anyone in business.

One call is all it took to set up a phone meeting with van Rensburg after the trade show. I had hoped it would just be the two of us on the phone, but when the call went through Deryck put me on speaker with Mike Ohmstede and Matthew Mitchell, two VEB executives I had gotten to know rather well.

I got straight to the point. I told him that I knew Zico was smaller than the companies VEB wanted to partner with but that because coconut water was developing so fast, they should reconsider that position. I said that we had the next round of investment all lined up and that now was the time for Coke to enter into the picture. I wasn't giving them the hard sell—these were just the facts as I knew them—but I did try to hint at a future that I knew they'd loathe.

"If I do this deal without you," I said, "you won't get another look at Zico for three or four years. By then we'll be twenty times the size and valuation and you won't be dealing with just me. I'll have a tough, pain-in-the-ass VC or private equity partner at my side setting the terms and conditions. Let's just sit down and see if there's anything here."

"Can you just hold on the line for a minute?" I heard Deryck say.

"Here is what we're going to do on our end," Deryck said when he came back on the line. "We're going to take a close look at Zico and try to get you a definitive answer about our interest soon. But in doing that we're going to research the whole category including your competitors. No promises about where we're going to come down."

"Fair enough," I said. "I'm confident that you are going to like what you see in Zico. The last thing I'd say to you is don't take too long. We're going to have to make a move with someone soon."

A few weeks later, I flew to Atlanta to give a full presentation to both the complete VEB staff and a few other Coke executives. Jim and I prepared hard for the meeting. The possibility existed that Coke was planning on launching their own brand or were already leaning toward partnering with a competing brand. In that case, all I was doing was giving them information that they would use to compete against me. I figured it was a risk that I'd have to take.

This was perhaps one of the most important presentations of my life, and though I'm often my own toughest critic, I nailed it. The mark of a great salesman is to be able to sell anything to anyone. I've never had that skill. However, when most people really believe in something, the way I believed in Zico, they can be very convincing. What made my pitch even more compelling was that I wasn't asking Coke to put a great deal at risk. We'd sign a contract that would give them a path to ownership and I'd use that relationship to bring in other financing for the company's near-term needs.

At dinner that night, Jim and I knew that we had nailed it. Our belief was confirmed a few weeks later when I got a call from Mike Ohmstede at VEB.

"Here's where we are," Mike said. "We looked at many options in the coconut water category and Zico is our leading contender. There are only two other options on the table. One is an internal play and the other is a real wild card option that has been brought to us by, well, let me just say, a friend of Coke's."

I told him that I was pretty sure I knew the options he was hinting at. The first, I said, was the possibility of launching a Jugos del Valle coconut water product since Coke had recently acquired that Mexican brand.

"Well," he said, "I can't confirm that."

"You and I know that's not going to work in this market, Mike. It's a Hispanic brand and not going to go mainstream. That's not a real option.

"That second option," I went on, "I'm going to guess is that the friend of Coke is someone who flies a lot of celebrities around in private jets. Jesse Itzler has come to you, hasn't he?"

"How do you know all this?" he said, now sounding a little paranoid.

"I do my homework, too, Mike," I told him. "I know this business and I've heard Jesse is a big fan of coconut water and looking to get in."

A few weeks later, I got another call from Mike confirming that Coke had picked Zico as the brand to partner with but they would only do it as the lead investor. There were a lot of details to be worked out, he told me. The executives above him were still concerned that Zico was small and that it needed some celebrity endorsers. Of course, Zico didn't have the money at that time to contract A-list celebrities or athletes, but with a major investment and Coke as a partner, I was confident we could figure it out. In pitching to Coke, Mike told me, Jesse had brought along a funny little home movie about a dad having to harvest coconuts from his backyard when his kids wanted a drink. The dad in his little home movie: Matt Damon. That got the attention of Coke executives and frankly mine, too.

"Are you telling me there's no deal if Jesse isn't involved?" I asked.

"No," he clarified. "I'm just telling you it's going to be easier to get it done with him involved, so you need to decide if you want to do that."

SKY-HIGH RAPPER

I knew Jesse's story. Among businesspeople in New York and beyond he was something of a legend. Though a serial entrepreneur he was most known for co-founding a private airline company, Marquis Jet, without bothering to own any planes or hire any pilots. He and his partner had the audacity to go to NetJets, a wholly owned subsidiary of Warren Buffett's Berkshire Hathaway group, and tell them they were missing a big opportunity. The bold, young entrepreneurs suggested using NetJets's planes, pilots, and infrastructure but selling the service under another name. The idea was so outrageously audacious as to be almost beyond belief. Imagine going to Ferrari and saying, "I'd like to sell your cars but I've got a different idea how to brand and market them."

NetJets was already doing great business selling shares in private jets. When once you had to come up with $40 million to own a private jet and millions per year to operate it, they made this luxury available "down market" to those who could afford only a fractional share in a jet. Jesse and his partner suggested to NetJets that they could bring in an even less rich crowd (say, a star athlete who had just signed a big contract or a B-list actor who was "only" making $2 million a year) by selling twenty-five-hour cards and marketing it under the name Marquis Jet so as not to dilute the rarefied NetJets brand.

Somehow they wrangled a meeting with Rich Santulli, the founder and CEO of NetJets. Santulli took a look at these twenty-something New Yorkers, the story goes, and escorted them to the door in under eight minutes. Remarkably, Itzler and his partner were undeterred and kept pressing the idea.

They did have something to bring to the table. Jesse had started out as a rapper and a music producer, and so he had access to up-and-coming celebrities in the New York scene. (If you want to transport yourself back to early 1990s pop-culture, check out his song "Shake It Like a White Girl" on YouTube.) To prove that, when he got another meeting with Santulli, he brought along members of Run-D.M.C. and former New York Giants star Carl Banks. Again Santulli passed but this time less forcefully. A half-dozen meetings later, Santulli consented to the partnership.

If Itzler wasn't already a hub of the New York in-crowd, his role in Marquis Jet made him into a celebrity among celebrities. Developing a marketing plan for the business was the first project on the nascent reality TV show *The Apprentice*, featuring none other than Donald Trump. The black Marquis Jet card became the status symbol among those with more status than they knew what to do with. He hung out with Gisele Bündchen, LeBron James, and the Knicks. LeBron spent time with Itzler at his lake house and Matt Damon flew with him to celebrity poker tournaments in Vegas. The mantra of Marquis was "Get in their lives." Jesse and the staff of Marquis made it their business to know the birthdays, anniversaries, preferences, and food allergies of all Marquis clients. As if that weren't enough to make Jesse the center of gravity among celebrity elite, he soon fell in love with and married Sara Blakely, founder of Spanx and hero to millions of women who didn't want panty lines to show through their pants. Jesse's Rolodex was legendary and, I was learning, something to be both respected and feared.

Celebrities—who have always held a spell over the American public—were growing in their power and influence. Big-name actors, musicians, and athletes have often been paid well but until rather recently, those making the real money off movies, concerts, and sporting events were the owners and businesses behind the scenes. That was changing. Celebrities were becoming increasingly savvy as businesspeople, and they were beginning to expect ownership stakes in both the public spectacles they starred in as well as in the products they endorsed.

More and more celebrities wanted in on the beverage action and their handlers, agents, and business managers were all looking to make deals. I met many of these supposed connectors. Vita Coco had retained one themselves, Guy Oseary. I knew we could do the same but perhaps Jesse could figure out how to do it more organically. After all, he was basically one of them now.

Jesse, I learned, was also an avid athlete and a serious distance runner, which was where his interest in the hydrating quality of coconut water was first sparked. The year before he had run a 100-mile road race with 135 other runners, using the event to raise money for charities. After a full twenty-four hours of running, fueled in part by Zico, Jesse placed in the top twenty-five, had run 100.8 miles, and had raised over a million dollars for charity. Recounting the achievement, *Newsday* called him a "marketing genius with a heart of gold."

He sounded like a guy to have on your side, so I called Mike from Coke back and said sure, let's give this a shot.

THREE-WAY DEAL

Not long after, we arranged a meeting in New York with Jesse, his key adviser, and Coke's VEB group's Matthew Mitchell and Mike Ohmstede. From the start, I could see Jesse's appeal. Tall, with curly blond hair and a big smile, he wore jeans, an old T-shirt, New Balance running shoes, and a headband—the same outfit I would see him in nearly every time. He had a style and coolness that seemed utterly his own.

The meeting was informal and Jesse impressed me with his genuine love of Zico and how much he knew about how we were building our business. According to Jesse, our efforts had netted dozens of celebrities and athletes as devoted customers.

"If we bring these names in as investors and figure out how to leverage them," Jesse told me, "I think we can use their affiliation to take Zico mainstream. I think it would be a blast to work with you and if we can be of help, I'm game for whatever works."

Matthew Mitchell commented, "Three-way deals are tough. We just need to be clear on a couple principles from Coke's side. First, you know we're not typical VC investors. We need to have some sort of path to ownership. Second, we're not going to pay twice: meaning we're not going to invest a huge amount, help build the brand, and then be expected to pay some exorbitant multiple at the end."

I interjected, "I get it, you don't want to repeat Vitaminwater. We'll figure out a way you can buy Zico someday for three billion dollars, not four." Everyone laughed.

"All right, just so everyone knows up front," Matthew continued. "Don't assume you get much from us early on. Distribution, marketing support, etc. All of that is really hard if not impossible when we're only minority investors."

I said, "Well, since you all laid out what you want, here's what I want. I want to see coconut water go mainstream across the world. I want to see Zico become one of the leading brands and stand for something good in the world. I want to see a major sustainable positive impact on the countries that grow coconuts. I want to give my investors, team, and my family a chance to benefit from all of this. And I'd love nothing more than to see Matt Damon drinking Zico in his next movie and see Coke make billions selling something healthy."

We all sat there for a few minutes trying to decide how to proceed. Finally David Moore, Jesse's adviser, said, "I think what we're all saying is it's your ball, your bat, your field, Mark; we just want to play ball. How can we be on the team?"

I took out a marker and started writing on a whiteboard.

"Let's sketch out what everyone wants and what each party can bring to the table. I need to raise $15 million to stay competitive and keep Zico front and center in this quickly growing category. Jesse, I know you're going to want something for joining and some upside. So we need to figure that out. You'll facilitate the opportunity for your celebrity friends to invest, but like you said earlier we need to reserve some equity for formal or informal endorsements.

"I think Coke should be in for half of the capital but no more at this point. Some of my investors are going to want to contribute more, and I'd like to give them a chance to do so.

"Coke is going to want some future rights to own it all so you'll have your path to ownership. But we need runway, autonomy, and the ability to make decisions on our own. I know you agree that if Coke tried to take over distributing and making deals for Zico, we're going to get lost in the machine. Within a few years, yes, but we agree you'll stay on the sideline at first."

The deal that eventually came together ended up looking very much like what we brainstormed together that day. Coke ended up investing the majority of the $15 million we raised, with Jesse, his friends and celebrities, and my existing investors contributing the difference.

The stakes were high. I knew that accepting Coke's help would eliminate a variety of other options. I knew that they would have the contractual right to buy us, when we hit certain sales figures, and that meant that there would be no IPO in my future and I wouldn't be handing the company down to my girls to run. There was the possibility that I might still run Zico under the auspices of Coke, but I would eventually be giving up ownership of the business I had spent the previous five years building.

In June of 2009 we signed a letter of intent with Coke that laid the groundwork for a three-way investment deal that would put $15 million behind Zico. The signing of that letter of agreement started a forty-five-day quiet period where all parties could evaluate the plan but no one could actively pursue other deals. For me, that meant not courting other investors or strategics, and for Coke it meant that they couldn't actively negotiate with Vita Coco or one of my other competitors.

In August of 2009, Jim Tonkin and I flew to Atlanta to work out the final details of the deal and structure. With so many players involved, we agreed to go on a communication lockdown to finish the deal. No cell phones or consulting with outside parties other than lawyers. We wanted to keep this as quiet as possible until we closed and could make an official announcement since rumors were already flying around about the pending deal.

On the second day we were making good progress and were about to break for lunch, when Mike Ohmstede of VEB came into the room.

"Have you seen the news?" he said. We looked up and shrugged. "This just came across the wire," he said as he handed around copies of a press release. I looked at the headline: "PepsiCo Agrees to Acquire Amacoco, Brazil's Largest Coconut Water Company." We all read in silence. Nowhere did the article mention that Amacoco was Zico's supplier. Indeed, if you couldn't read between the lines, you'd think that Pepsi was just getting into the coconut water business for the sole reason that it was profitable in South America. Already highlighted and circled was this statement: "PepsiCo will build on the existing network and will utilize the strength of its local distribution system to expand sales across Brazil, as well as to other markets worldwide."

Instead of buying into an existing brand, PepsiCo had taken another strategy. Apparently, they wanted to first lock down a key supplier. With that leverage, they could launch their own brand or buy into an existing one with greater control. Indeed it was only a few weeks later that they announced their investment in ONE coconut water. I had to admit, it was a pretty smart move, but it assumed supply was the critical element to success and I wasn't sure that was the case.

"Now what's going to happen?" one of the Coke lawyers asked. "Mark, you have a two-year contract with Amacoco, right? That gives you plenty of time to figure it out."

"Realistically," I told them, "they'll come through on the orders in the pipeline and that means we're good through the first quarter of 2010. After that they'll turn us off like a garden hose."

"So you'll have to sue them to keep to their contract?" suggested one of the lawyers.

"The chances of a good outcome suing a company for breach of contract in Brazil is next to zero," I told them. I had enough experience with business deals in Central and South America to know that was a dead end. "It will take too long and there is a good possibility that we'll lose. Either way, it's just not worth the effort."

There were some nervous glances around the room. With the contract with Coke just hours from being signed, I wasn't going to allow this news to ruin the deal.

"I've been clear from the start that this was always a possibility," I said. "Coconuts are grown and processed all around the world. I've visited and kept up discussions with dozens of other suppliers in

Thailand, Indonesia, and the Philippines. With the operational resources of Coke, getting a quality, secure, cost-effective supply of
young coconut water will not be a problem."

When the Coke team left the room for a break, Jim and I were
silent for a moment.

"So Pepsi buying Amacoco was no big deal?" he asked, smiling.
"You really that calm and confident?"

"Hell no," I said, picking up the press release and reading it again.
"It's true that we did see this coming, but I didn't think it would happen so soon. We're not ready to find a new supply in the next few
months. Not without Coke behind us. If they walk at this point, we'll
figure it out but it's not going to be easy."

With the final contract ironed out, I had a few weeks to hold my
breath to see if the Coke board would approve it. I put the odds in my
favor but I knew that Pepsi's purchase of Amacoco would weigh heav-
ily on their minds. I also knew from friendly insiders at Coke that Vita
Coco was basically calling every number in the Coke phone directory
to see if they could get in front of the deal. "Those guys are persistent,"
I had been told. "They are calling all over the building. They're all
freaking out." I had to assume Coke had been in discussions with
them for some time while they were exploring all the brands in the
category.

I definitely wanted to nail down a partnership with Coke and beat
out Vita Coco for that spot. While I worried that partnering with a
large bureaucracy might be an encumbrance, the advantages of having one of the largest organizations on earth as your partner were
huge, I hoped. Distribution was of course one of the biggest challenges any consumer product has and Coke, I had to assume, would
eventually help with that. So, too, with food science, product development, building a global supply chain, and of course marketing. Getting my phone calls returned would no longer be an issue.

But the Amacoco purchase or some other internal issue could still come up to sabotage the plan potentially, and Coke could deep-six the deal. During those weeks I talked with Maura about our options. If Coke passed, I'd still be in the fight. In fact, the potential long-term upside for our personal wealth would be substantially higher. We'd keep a larger ownership share, go back to the venture capital world, and have the potential to lead Zico toward a possible IPO or billion-dollar sale. With every month, more investment capital was looking for a home, and our alliance with Coke would attract plenty of interest even if the relationship was never consummated. In fact, both Jim and I had been contacted by one of the firms that earlier turned us down. Neither of us spoke with them, respecting our agreement with Coke, but the voice mail was clear: "We may have missed our chance but we'd really love to back Zico any way we can."

The Coke partnership was the safer bet, albeit the one that limited the high-end payoffs. My tolerance for risk remained pretty robust, but this was no longer just about me. I thought back on all the difficulties and near disasters I had asked Maura and my family (not to mention my early investors and employees) to weather over the last five years, and I knew it was time to take the safer route. The deal with Coke would bring a measure of stability to our lives and those of the Zico team. Roller coasters are a thrill until you've been riding one for a number of years.

Zico was heading down the route of many of the entrepreneurial brands I respected most. Burt's Bees sold to Clorox. Ben & Jerry's sold to Unilever. Tom's of Maine sold to Colgate. Honest Tea was on a similar path with Coke. In all these cases, loyal consumers feared this meant the death of these innovative brands. These entrepreneurs weren't just selling, many would assume, they were "selling out." I knew some Zico fans would have the same concerns. But what is poorly understood by the average consumer is that these huge companies aren't simply buying what is sometimes called "the face of the brand." The value of entrepreneurial brands doesn't exist in the name or the founder alone but in the product itself and all the ways the smaller company has acted in the world. The large companies that buy these eccentric brands know that for their purchase to retain its value, they have to uphold and manifest the virtues that brought the company into prominence. Upstart brands can change capitalism not only by competing with the old guard but also by joining forces with them. At the end of the day, my goal was not simply to have Zico in the hands of yoga moms and Whole Foods shoppers. I wanted it available at Target, Walmart, and in truck stops and school soda machines. I wanted it available every place you could buy a Coke. And who better to help us do that than Coke itself?

When the news came that Coke had approved the deal, everyone in the industry heard about it within the day. The general consensus was that Zico had won the coconut water wars and all that was left were the details. How could we lose with such a major player backing us?

I definitely appreciated the congratulations rolling in from every quarter, but I knew for certain that the story was far from over. Coke's full buyout of Zico wasn't certain, only a contractual option. In fact, to make that buyout attractive to Maura, me, and all our early investors, Zico would have to hit some ambitious sales targets over the next few years. Whether the $15 million would give us the ammunition to make those targets was far from guaranteed. Vita Coco certainly wasn't waiting around to see what happened. CEO Mike Kirban released a statement later that week saying he turned down Coke's offer to invest millions and said, "Am I worried? Not really." Within a few months he also announced a distribution agreement with Dr Pepper Snapple Group. They were smaller than Coke or Pepsi, but had a reputation of being more flexible and scrappy, sort of like Exclusive in

New York. Now the coconut water wars were moving to a new level. They were now becoming proxy wars between beverage superpowers.

By September 2009, we had finalized our deal with Coke, Jesse Itzler, and other investors, and we had $15 million in our company bank account. After running a company whose account was often near zero for almost five years, the investment seemed like a fortune. For most companies (at least those not in the overheated tech economy), it is a fortune. Better still, unlike previous financing rounds, this one came in immediately, not in dribs and drabs over months. We received big, fat wire transfers all on the same day. It was easy and fun to fantasize about how we might spend that on building the Zico brand.

But I reminded myself that I had seen beverage companies burn through that amount of cash and more in just a few years. My friends Eric and Steve at Steaz tea had raised $11 million from a prominent VC firm in 2008. They were passionate founders, had a great brand with strong products, and solid initial distribution. They invested heavily in field sales and marketing teams and branded vehicles up and down the East Coast to launch a series of major distributors. But the volume just did not come as quickly as they expected, and within two years they were nearly broke. They survived thanks to some quick cost cutting and by refocusing on natural foods, but the founders lost control of their company in the process.

Similarly, Purple Beverage Company came out of nowhere in 2007, trying to become the next POM Wonderful by selling a blend of juices supposed to be high in antioxidants. They took an unconventional public market angle to raise $10 million or more and at one point in 2008 were valued at $180 million. They invested hard and fast, including launching Big Geyser with a sales blitz team of more than twenty. The move looked promising. They sold ten thousand cases to retailers during their launch week in New York, which led me to ask, "Am I doing the right thing with this disciplined and methodical approach?" I got my answer within a few weeks when I learned that seven thousand of those cases were returned because they didn't sell. By the end of 2009, the company was effectively shut down and investors were left holding an empty bag.

Around the same time, Adina beverages, which had been a small regional beverage company in San Francisco, came under the wing of the legendary founder of Odwalla, Greg Steltenpohl. They subsequently raised $14 million from a who's who list of investors and VC firms and installed none other than John Bello as CEO, the founder and former CEO for SoBe Beverages. Bello had all but created the enhanced beverage category in the 1990s. Within two years they'd burned through all their cash and shut their doors.

If that could happen to these entrepreneurs, all of whom were more experienced than me, I had to be cautious. Everyone, including Zico, was hoping to be the next Vitaminwater, and being an entrepreneur requires a certain amount of risk taking, but it's also dangerous to believe your own hype.

So we would be aggressive strategically and cautious financially, but at least we would be doing it all from sunny California. Earlier that spring, after years of considering options all over the country, Maura and I settled on Los Angeles as the place to open a real non-garage office. We found and leased a converted warehouse space in Hermosa Beach. I felt I knew New York well enough to manage it from afar, and strategically I was certain that California was fertile ground to grow the Zico brand. When the Big Geyser team got wind of the decision they were not thrilled. They worried we would lose our focus on New York. Leaving Buck Willams behind, who knew New York best of all, calmed their nerves somewhat.

But the reality was, this move was personal. I had given Maura my commitment that within five years we'd move to somewhere she wanted to live. This adventure was far from over, and I needed to know she and the girls were happy and grounded to do what I needed to do. By the time our deal with Coke closed, we had moved ourselves and settled in Redondo Beach, just a bike ride away from the office. It was time to move into the sunshine.

CHAPTER 10

YOU CAN'T LOSE WHEN YOU'VE ALREADY WON

After the 2009 announcement of Coke's investment, some of my friends and relatives assumed that we'd simply start loading blue cases onto those ubiquitous red trucks and suddenly Zico would appear in every cooler and the beverage aisle in every store in the country and beyond. Both the VEB team and I believed that Zico was still much too small to survive in the Coke distribution system, let alone thrive. We agreed on a revenue target, assuming it was good-quality revenue (focused on limited markets and channels) that would be the right point to begin to integrate Zico into the Coke system.

Until then our team would be completely in the driver's seat, which was a good thing. We were in a street fight with our coconut water competitors—an all-out battle for the hearts and minds of retailers and customers alike. Vita Coco was already leveraging their relationship with Dr Pepper Snapple Group (DPSG) to begin to scale nationwide. Coke's conventional weapons, including their infrastructure, traditional advertising, and distribution system, were more cumbersome than DPSG's and even the largest of battleships. It could not be turned on a dime to focus on little Zico. Our objective became clear: to grow the brand mostly through non-Coke channels over the next three to four years as we learned how Zico might plug into the Coke system when the time was right.

Jesse and his team soon began to kick into gear. Kelly Ripa showed up in gossip pages with a Zico in hand. Amare Stoudemire was drinking Zico at a press conference to announce he was signing a hundred-million-dollar deal to play for the Knicks. Then Lauren Conrad was at an outdoor café in L.A., Courteney Cox on a movie set, Ellen Pompeo getting into an SUV after a workout—all holding Zicos. Boston Celtic Kevin Garnett was quoted saying how critical Zico was to his performance. I never exactly knew whether Jesse was responsible for these seemingly unintentional celebrity endorsements, but I was always happy with the buzz and excitement they brought. My favorite photo of the bunch may have been Gisele Bündchen valiantly fending off the intrusion of a paparazzi's camera by shielding her face with a bottle of Zico in hand—label facing the camera of course.

Jesse was able to get living legend Walt Frazier to pay a visit to the Big Geyser annual distributor meeting and leveraged his Marquis Jet connections to help us charter a private jet to fly some top-selling distributors to a Patriots versus Jets game in Boston. That got their attention. If nothing else, Jesse was making everything at Zico even more fun.

I had heard through the grapevine that Alex Rodriguez was an avid Zico fan a few years earlier, so I was not surprised to learn that he was part of the group that invested in Zico with Jesse. Jesse got him to do a little video talking about how much he loved Zico, encouraging the Big Geyser sales reps to sell it everywhere.

Jesse said A-Rod and his agent wanted to discuss him becoming an official spokesperson for Zico—a service that certainly would come with a big price tag in cash or equity in the company. A-Rod was handsome, a great ball player, and one of the most famous athletes in the country. In 2009, however, he had tarnished his on-field heroics by admitting to steroid use, and around the same time his marriage was destroyed when he was connected romantically with Madonna. The guy was a hot mess and not exactly a poster child for the all-natural image we were trying to portray. I told Jesse that, while I was happy to have A-Rod as a consumer and investor, I wasn't going to give him extra money or equity to publically endorse our brand.

My mistake was that I thought I could take the benefits of Rodriguez without much risk. I accepted his investment in Zico and was pleased when rumors got around that we were delivering cases of Zico to Yankee stadium at the request of the team's biggest star.

But then things got a little crazy. Madonna, it turns out, was an investor in Vita Coco and an active public endorser of the product. And Madonna's business partner Guy Oseary also happened to be A-Rod's manager. Of course, I'm not sure what sort of conversation happened between Madonna and A-Rod or in what situation, but suddenly Rodriguez was publically endorsing Vita Coco.

The press had a field day. "Alex Rodriguez looked like a nut yesterday after backing two rival coconut water brands," wrote the *New York Post*. "Error on the Play: A-Rod Endorses Vita Coco While Investing in Its Biggest Competitor," said *Sports Business Daily*. *USA Today* had the most insightful take, pointing to the dangers inherent in having celebrities as investors. "The coconut water craziness shows what can go amiss when a growing business takes money from a 'celebrity' investor. . . . Typically, only company insiders know the details when a problem arises with low-profile investors. But when a famous name is involved, it can quickly become public fodder."

That *USA Today* reporter had it right, but the truth was that the A-Rod dustup was only a minor setback. For the most part, the celebrities who embraced our brand were very much aligned with our own motivations and intentions. Nearly all were interested in putting their names and influence behind products that they believed in and moved the dial toward health, sustainability, and social good. With few exceptions, they weren't just out to make a buck but to make the world a better place by degrees.

CLIMBING TO THE TOP

The next two years were a whirlwind. Sales continued to grow at a strong clip through Big Geyser in New York and with the help of broker Presence Marketing in natural foods. We built out our team to replicate the powerful New York model in other markets across the country. We also closed a deal with Trader Joe's that boosted our volume significantly. Our team and sales consultants L.A. Libations got Zico into select regions of Target, Costco, 7-Eleven, and other major chains. Our test of Zico in Coke's Los Angeles market showed that the brand could work within their system with the right focus, attention, and alignment. Our sales skyrocketed past everyone's expectation even though less than 10 percent of our sales went through the Coke system.

As this happened, I traveled around the world to shore up our supply lines and ensure that we'd never be at the mercy of a single supplier. I made deals in Thailand, Indonesia, and the Philippines. Once again, in choosing whom to work with, I relied less on external certifications than I did on my own assessment of the working conditions and the owners' values. I make no claim that this was a foolproof process, but I believe I developed an increasingly keen instinct for assessing the ethics of other businesspeople and their organizations.

Sharing the bounty of the growing American market for coconut water in communities where it had a meaningful impact on the population's standard of living was a great feeling. I remember a woman named Khun Nam in Thailand who ran a multi-generational coconut farm at the time I met her. Within a year, our purchases allowed her to hire fifty additional workers at good wages and upgrade her processing plant so that it could pass Coke's stringent quality standards.

In October of 2011, I was back in Hermosa Beach in a meeting with the sales staff when Candace Crawford, our CFO, knocked on the door.

"I have some news you're going to want to hear right now," she said. I excused myself and went to her office.

"The sales numbers for October are in," she said. Her expression was all business but I could tell that she was either going to tell me really good news or really bad news. "Last month we did over six million dollars in sales. That brings our total for the last twelve months to almost forty million dollars."

Then she smiled and gave me a high five. That number was critical because it was well above the figure that opened up the possibility Coke would increase its stake in Zico and we would begin discussions about full distribution in their system. I had predicted that it would take us three to four years from signing the Coke deal to reach this point. We had done it in less than two.

A few months later, I made my annual pilgrimage to the Natural Products Expo West show in Anaheim, California. I had attended the show with Zico each year since 2005, our first full year in business. It had always been a critical place to meet buyers and industry leaders, to show new products and sign up new retailers. We had, as usual, a beautiful booth with a gorgeous blue background, white floor, and countertop, all reminiscent of a tropical spa. We had a team of sales, marketing, and office staff manning the booth, and there was more excitement and energy than ever.

Only a few weeks earlier, industry veteran reporter Gerry Khermouch had written a story speculating that Coke was finalizing a deal to purchase a controlling interest in Zico. That was followed by a *Wall Street Journal* article that stated the same. As the rumor circulated, I found that I had become a minor celebrity at the trade show—even beyond the typical beverage set. I was getting congratulated and high-fived by people I'm pretty sure I'd never met. Others cornered me at every opportunity to ask how I had done it. Sticking to the confidentiality agreement, I demurred, but I'm sure my face gave it all away. It was a big deal and everyone including myself now expected Coke to put its real muscle behind the Zico brand and eventually scale fast, become the number one brand, and buy all of our remaining stake. The finish line was in sight. I'd have happy employees, ecstatic investors, and a relieved wife.

I still enjoyed working the Zico booth, but I also took the time to walk the showroom floor. I remembered being awed by the creativity on display at the Fancy Food Show in New York when I first joined this industry. Now, eight years later, the spirit of entrepreneurship in the beverage and food sector of the American economy was only growing. Here were entrepreneurs set on changing the world for the better. Few would survive but I loved the passion and potential displayed on this trade show floor and hoped someday I might help them avoid some of my mistakes.

"So now you're working for big red," a Coke person I vaguely knew said, slapping me on the back and startling me out of my reverie. "Welcome to the big league!" I'm sure he meant it as a compliment but I wasn't sure I liked the sound of it. Being a smaller player in this dynamic world had been challenging and exciting, and I wasn't sure I wanted to give that up.

BIG RED AND LITTLE BLUE

Once the Coke ownership of the majority of Zico had become official, we could plan for a national rollout. Coke's eventual 100 percent purchase of Zico wasn't guaranteed but seemed all but inevitable. Now that we were going to put the full force of the Coke system behind us, we believed the brand would scale even faster. But no one expected it to be an easy transition and it certainly wasn't.

We knew from past experiences it would take time. Coke took a few years to get it right with Smartwater, which is now a massively successful brand. Same with Honest Tea, which was now in one hundred thousand outlets and growing by leaps and bounds. Big companies move slowly, and the efficiencies that they offer can't be turned on like a switch, which is one of the reasons why it is difficult to introduce small brands into any large corporate structure.

Though we had our challenges, I was impressed that nearly everyone I worked with at Coke seemed truly thrilled to be working on a product that they knew was healthy and good for the world. I knew they were as committed as the Zico team to figuring out how to make it work. Over the next year, Coke would help us increase our store count from roughly fifteen thousand to more than thirty thousand, continuing to add more every year. The Zico operations team figured out how to scale production in a massive way and develop an impressive pipeline of innovations. The Zico and VEB marketing teams would launch the amazing new "Crack Life Open" marketing campaign anchored around Jessica Alba. Our field sales and marketing teams would figure out how to build the Zico brand in markets across the country.

By the fall of 2013, I realized that if we were going to fully capitalize on the massive opportunity in front of us, we needed to solidify our relationship. Coke needed to make a decision: would they buy Zico or not? Though contractually they had the option to do so in another year or two, I worried that if we waited that long, we would miss out on the full potential of the brand. As a semi-independent company, we just wouldn't be able to continue to invest the amount of money required with Vita Coco continuing to raise more and more capital and scaling fast in DPSG's system.

I decided it was time to bring this to a head and have a serious conversation about what to do next. In a meeting in Atlanta I told the Coke team that in order to stay competitive with other brands, Zico would require more investment and a more aggressive strategy than the cash available from our current deal with Coke would allow.

I spelled out three scenarios to deal with the situation. I would either get the autonomy and the resources to swing for the fences in a fast-moving market, or Coke could buy us now and get the full benefit from their additional investment in the brand. If Coke really didn't believe in Zico, then I was prepared to raise the money to buy them out. All the scenarios would benefit the brand we had worked so hard to build.

The Coke team agreed with my assessment and needed a few weeks to consider all their options. I presented no bluffs. I was ready to make good on any of the options. What I was not willing to do was see the Zico brand unable to realize its true potential. What would Coke choose? I had done my part. I had spent nine years to get to this point. From here forward it was providence, and I was ready to accept whatever lay in front of me.

WE ALREADY WON

Business books, like history books, are written by the winners. But what does it mean to win in this day and age? When and how do you know you've won? Here's the conventional story of how we won: it happened the evening of November 20, 2013, when I received word that Coke had officially bought Zico.

A little after six on an exceptionally warm evening, I was driving past the office buildings and small shopping complexes on Aviation Boulevard on the way from Zico's offices to my family home in Redondo Beach. The dashboard monitor on my high-tech little Toyota

Prius announced the call from my CFO/COO Candace, and although I already suspected what she had to tell me, I could feel my heart rate jump. After a tense and difficult negotiation, Coke had opted to accelerate their full buyout of Zico. Never had I played for higher stakes. My palms sweat to recall critical moments, but a deal had been agreed to that I felt was fair to us, our investors, and our mission. All that was left was for a very large amount of money to be wired into the Zico bank account.

"Hello," I said in a voice that I hoped sounded calm and optimistic.

"It's done," Candace told me with no preamble. "Just got confirmation from our bank that the wire left their bank already. It will be in our account in the morning."

Fearing that the gods of irony might be in a mischievous mood, I found a safe place to pull over. That a fortune the size of a multistate lottery was hovering somewhere in cyberspace on the way to Zico's bank account was big news for me but also, I knew, for Candace and so many others. "All I can say right now is thank you for helping me navigate through this," I said after a pause. "Go have some fun and I'll see you in the morning. I'd really like you to be there in person for the conference call tomorrow." She and I both understood that we still had a lot to do. We had to tell the Zico staff and begin the integration process. I was looking forward to the substantial checks I was going to get to sign for every employee and all the patient and supportive investors who included many family members and friends. No doubt about it, big changes were coming to a lot of people, myself included.

After disconnecting the call, I sat there on the side of the road and thought about the journey we had been on. Over the last ten years we had been through so much: the adrenaline rush of our launch, the dark times teetering near bankruptcy, massive swings in fortune as we struggled to create a stable supply chain in developing countries, the uncertainty at times if our health, marriage, and sanity would weather the storms.

Money is our culture's most common metric for success. But it's too simple a scorecard. Money may make for a compelling story but it certainly does not guarantee a fulfilling life. Sitting on the side of the road as the sun settled down on the Pacific Ocean, I knew already that I had a different story I wanted to tell.

The honest truth is that I had never only measured my success creating Zico solely by the numbers, whatever they might be: growth rate, market capitalization, market share, IPO valuation, sale price, or the size of my personal bank account. Of course, I did pay attention to the numbers and was more than happy to know my bank account would include a few more zeros at the end. For those who become addicted to that game, however, no number is high enough. The sale to Coke was a case in point. Even though I had landed a significant fortune—enough to provide my family with financial independence indefinitely—I knew others would wonder if I should have gone bigger. Should I have held on to the company, angled for an IPO, gone for *billions*?

Let me give you a thought experiment: Let's say you are at the beginning of starting a business and you suddenly have the power to see the future. What you can see down the road, say, after ten years of hard work, is the business does just okay—nothing close to the rip-roaring success you had dreamed of. The question is this: would you still invest your time, talent, and treasure in that business?

The idea that you might answer that question with an enthusiastic "yes!" might puzzle many old-school business thinkers. Certainly, with your magical foreknowledge, you'd place a more promising bet with your time and energy. But what this sort of thinking ignores is the value inherent in the journey—the experiences, personal growth, and happiness that happen along the way. The impact you can make on other people's lives. I believe that if you pick the right product or service that's aligned with your highest and best use and imbue your business with your personal values, passions, and philosophy, those ten years will represent one of the best decades of your life regardless of the zero or zeros in your bank statement.

The flipside to this thought experiment is: Suppose again that you can see the future of your business and a true pot of gold awaits you ten years down the road. But to get there you learn that you'd have to sacrifice your marriage, give up a meaningful relationship with your children, betray devoted employees, take advantage of impoverished populations, and damage the environment. Very few of us are socio-pathic enough to make that sort of deal up front. The sad truth is that in retrospect, this is the bargain that many businesspeople end up making. Let me state the obvious: It's a bad deal. No amount of money is worth a decade of incrementally losing your soul.

So how did I know I had won? Let me tell you another story that happened on the same day I got the phone call that the deal with Coke was done. It took place just a half hour later when I got home to my family. Maura was cooking a simple but typical dinner of black beans, rice, and salad, and our younger daughter, Lexi, was finishing her homework at the kitchen table. Our older daughter, Ciara, would still need to be picked up from gymnastics in an hour and it was my turn to do so. Of course, I told Maura the news and she threw her arms around my neck enthusiastically and screamed with joy.

I'll remember that evening mostly for our simple family dinner together. Not all business entrepreneurs are so lucky on the day they cash out. Some go out to thousand-dollar meals with expensive wine but come home alone to large, empty houses. The fact that I had my family beside me for the entire journey and that we were eating the same meal we've had a hundred times, was certainly an indication that I had won and, in fact, had been winning all along.

So had we sold out? If our goal was to run Zico independently forever and pass it on to our kids, then perhaps. But that was never our goal. Had we sold too soon? If my goal was to be a centa-millionaire or billionaire or king of the coconut water world then, again, perhaps.

After dinner, Maura and I cleaned up as we finished a bottle of wine and talked through the last ten years. We toasted to this big milestone and breathed a sigh of relief. We also discussed regrets—both the ones we already had and those that we might have in the future. Our learning curve had been so steep along the way that mistakes were inevitable, and we made many. And we had so many ideas yet to implement, especially on the social and environmental impact side of the equation.

Letting go of Zico was hard, and trusting Coke with the brand that we had cultivated and nurtured was certainly a gamble. Would they know how to maintain and grow it? Our dream was that in selling Zico to Coke we'd begun a change for that company—that they would use their massive production, distribution, and marketing power to begin to deliver a healthy beverage to populations around the world. That would be a public health coup of major proportions, but it remained to be seen if they would pull it off. How would they treat employees and suppliers down to the farmers and what would happen to them? Would they continue to factor in the environmental impact of Zico? It was all uncertain. But what I believed was that fundamentally the people at Coke wanted to do the right thing and that the Zico brand and team that would continue to run it were strong enough to survive and thrive in that environment and keep the brand values intact.

Putting the what-ifs aside, we talked about the lessons we had learned about starting a business and creating a brand in a rapidly changing business climate. In a decade we had established Zico as an icon-in-the-making brand and been one of the first to market in what was on its way to being a multibillion-dollar new global category. We had helped disrupt the beverage industry that had for over a century relied on selling caffeinated sugar water in endless varieties and flavors. We had laid a foundation upon which dozens of entrepreneurs were building perhaps even better brands and businesses. We had made a positive contribution to the health of millions and spurred massive and sustainable economic development in numerous poor countries. We had given ourselves and our team of employees the opportunity to learn, contribute, and grow. We created a brand that stood for something good in the world and delivered authentic value by looking within our own lives to discover what was important to us. As our reward, we now had the know-how and financial resources to help other entrepreneurs on their quests, and many of them were taking the concept of reaching higher to a whole new level.

Standing in front of a piece of fine craftsmanship or a piece of art, you can sense the human passion and joy that went into the creation. I believe that businesses and brands today should be no different. Like many other entrepreneurs, I discovered that consumers, investors, employees, and partners respond enthusiastically to products and brands when the passion, personality, and enthusiasm of another person shine through. If you reach higher and pursue a venture that is deeply personal, bigger than just you, and is close to your highest and best self, you cannot lose, and the world will be better for your having done so. That is reaching higher and that is revolutionary.

ACKNOWLEDGMENTS

Like everything important I've ever accomplished in my life, including founding and building Zico, completing this book was the result of the effort of many, many people. There is simply no way I could have done it alone and also no way to recognize everyone involved, but I do want to mention a few. Thanks to their support, encouragement, dedication, and occasional kick in the rear, it all came together better than I could have hoped.

First and foremost, I want to thank Adrian Zackheim, my brilliant publisher. He saw something in me and my story and coaxed and prodded me until I found that kernel of truth that became the basis for *High-Hanging Fruit*. Stephanie Frerich, my charming and talented editor, believed in me much more than I did myself at times and had just the right balance of positive encouragement to keep me writing and tough love when it came to delivering a readable book fit for publication. Pilar Queen, my incredible agent, saw potential in my story before nearly anyone else and fought hard, even against me sometimes, to keep its integrity and ensure the final product was the best I could produce.

Lisa Tenner's writing course and consultations helped me begin the long process of finding my voice. I owe special thanks to my writing coach, Ethan Watters. His patient prodding, spot-on suggestions, and tireless dedication not only helped me understand and use language, tone, structure, flow, and the art of storytelling: he helped me fall in love with writing.

After reading this book, there should be no doubt about the role my wonderful wife, Maura, played in Zico and my life. So, too, in this book. Her encouragement and support, memory, countless edits and discussions, ego-popping challenges, and reminders to follow my own advice about staying sane and enjoying the ride helped me do both and deliver the best book I could. My beautiful daughters, Ciara and Lexi, were an inspiration from the beginning and always remind me what's really important in life. They and so many in their generation give me hope for the screwy yet awe-inspiring world they will inherit.

My parents, siblings, and extended family have always believed in me, and knowing they would forever welcome me back into the family fold allowed me to take off on wild journeys, including this book. Special mention to my sister, Mary Beth, who has been one of my best friends and inspirations since my first memories and was so much a part of the Zico and *High-Hanging Fruit* journey.

Maura's family, the Smiths, played an equally important role, taking me as one of their own and supporting and encouraging Maura and me on our wild adventures. Special thanks to Barb for being one of the earliest believers in Zico and Gerry for being a true life mentor and pushing me hard to make sure this book would not be a "thud."

I certainly need to thank all the Zico team, past, present, and future, in the U.S. and around the world. There are so many that my editor would not allow me to mention you all, but thanks to your and your families' and significant others' passion, sense of ownership, and commitment to making the Zico brand your own, you made it so much more than I ever could have done alone. Special thanks to the Lead Team in its various iterations, especially Candace Crawford, Chris Weavers, Bill Lange, and Mike Sharman. Also to the sales and marketing "dirty dozen" who came aboard when Zico was barely out of kindergarten and stuck around to help build it into the powerhouse brand it was meant to become: Andrew Griffiths, Rory Mulcahy, Andrew Giardino, Carlos Ramirez, Michael "Buck" Williams, Katie Journey, T. J. Leenders, Jeff Seavey, Matt Rothschild, Juliet Kim, Treva McCroskey, and Michelle McKinney. Then there is the earliest Zico team, circa 2004: Roberto Ruiz, Jose Gonzalez, Chris Michaels, Juan Gutierrez, Jhonnie Ospina, and James Heslop. You laid the foundation and early momentum that got it all started.

Thanks to Jesse Itzler, Marc Adelman, Jennifer Kish, Brian Black, Adam Padilla, and the rest of the Suite 850/100-mile man team. I loved your drive, creativity, and determination and only wish we had a chance to really show the world what we could do together over a longer term.

I want to thank the nearly one hundred investors in Zico. Without your belief in me and Zico and providing your precious resources, encouragement, and support again and again, Zico would simply not exist.

Thank you to those on the various iterations of Zico's board of advisors and directors for your guidance and support, including Jack Belsito, Peter Brodsky, Marie Quintero Johnson, Wendy Clark, Ron Lewis, Deryck van Rensburg, and especially consigliere extraordinaire and dear friend Jim Tonkin. You all pushed me to be better and always helped me do what was right for the business and brand.

There are many I want to thank in the yoga community but I can't possibly mention them all. I do want to make special mention of Jen

Lobo, Donna Rubin, Karima and David Wilner, Mark Drost, Otto Cedeño, Tricia Donegan, Darius Le Gall, Mardina Chen, Najla Barile, and all their staff, teachers, and students over the years. Your support of Zico helped us immensely, as did you welcoming Maura and me into your community. Then there are the many celebrities, athletes, nutritionists, trainers, and other influencers including the many iterations of Team Zico. Thank you for putting your time, support, and reputation behind Zico.

There are so many in the beverage industry to thank, but once again I can't possibly mention them all. First, a very special thanks to the Hershkowitz family, Lewis, Lynn, and Stephen, as well as Jerry Reda, Dan Reade, and the whole Big Geyser team over the years. You challenged me and my team to make Zico the best it could be and stuck with us when we failed again and again. Special thanks to Harold Baron and especially Irving "Hal" Hershkowitz (may they both rest in peace). Big H reared so many brands and made a huge and lasting impact on our industry. We all owe him a debt of gratitude. Thanks as well to Tony Haralambos, Ralph Crowley, Scott Beim, Marc Kramer, Gary Poos, Gary Rezeppa, John Blair, John Keaneally, Tom and Scott LeBon, Brad Barnhorn, Greg Horn, John Sicher, John Craven, Jeff Klineman, Michael Bellas, Bruce Klion, Bob and Bill Sipper, Bob Corsaro, Tom DeLucca, Richard Hall, Ross Colbert, Andrew Kaplan, and their respective organizations and teams. Also special thanks to Gerry Khermouch for fact-checking and editing certain elements of this book. I learned so much from each of you and would have a very different story to tell without your help, support, and guidance.

There were so many great beverage entrepreneurs that went before me and helped and inspired me over the years. Don Vultaggio, Rodney Sachs, Mark Hall, Darius Bikoff, Mike Repole, Lance Collins, Tom Scott, Tom First, Seth Goldman, Todd Woloson, John

Bello, Greg Steltenpohl, and Jimmy Rosenberg among them. You laid the foundation on which Zico and every new beverage brand is built. Thank you for what you did.

To what I'll call the New Age Beverage Class of the early 2000s: Ryan and Jeremy Black, Clayton Christopher, David Smith, Kara and Theo Goldin, Eric Schnell, Steve Kessler, Chris Cuvelier, Alex Pryor, David Karr, and Steve Hersh among many others. I learned so much from you fighting for shelf space, sharing war stories, watching successes and failures. Special thanks to Mike Kirban and Ira Liran from Vita Coco and Rodrigo Veloso from ONE and their incredible teams. Yes, I wanted to crush you and I know you felt the same, but in hindsight I'm thankful for worthy competitors that kept me on my toes and made me and our whole team better.

There were so many organizations that helped Zico in sales, marketing, legal, accounting, and other services over the years and I can only highlight a few: Bill Weiland and team at Presence Marketing. Danny Stepper, Dino Sarti, Pat Bolden and the crew at L.A. Libations. Colin Jones, David Johnson, and everyone at Omni Partners. Josh Wand and team from BevForce. Tom Aarts, Grant Ferrier, and the Nutrition Capital Network. Mark Denusak and team at Commerce House. John Butler, Greg Stern, Patrick Kiss, and all at Butler, Shine. Eric Johnson and team at Ignited. Sandy Hillman, Alison Brod, Rob Bratskeir, and their respective teams. Mara Engle, Sheryl Roth, and crew at Organic Works. Alan, Eddie, and team at Phoenix Warehouse. Jon Vaccaro and the Bettaway organization. Marc Press, Barry Schwartz, and team at Cole Schotz; Vincent Bacchetta and Company; Alon Haim and team at Citizens Bank.

Many hundreds and soon to be thousands of people at The Coca-Cola Company in the U.S., Europe, Asia, and Latin America have dedicated incredible amounts of time, effort, and true passion to scale Zico, and I can't thank you enough. The list would be incredibly long but I do want to give special mention to the Ventures and Emerging Brands team, especially Deryck van Rensburg, Scott Uzzell, Matthew Mitchell, Mike Ohmstede, Matt Hughes, Tom Larson, Darren Marshall, Rebecca Messina, Mark Kelsey, Wadhi Khayat, Lorna Peters, Sarah Hutton, Mary Ann Somers, and Debbie Bachman. It gives me great pleasure to know such a dedicated team is now taking Zico to the next level in hands more capable than mine.

So many other individuals helped me and Zico over the years and there are a few I'd like to highlight: Perry Abbenante, Geoff Abbott, Dr. Peter Adams, Leonard Armato, Lara Bandler Hogan, Tim Barton, Eric Bechtel, Jay and Nancy Benkovich, Sara Blakely, Phillip Boyle, Andy Burger, Juan Pablo Cappello, Rocky Clause, Rodney Cohen, Joe Desena, Dr. Michael DiGeronimo, Carolla Dost, Jake Fontenot, Katherine Gehls, Gil Greene, Mike Guidry, Ken Haubein, Palo Hawken, Chris Hoemeke, Dustin Hopper, Jake Jacobs, Marc Joubert, Scott Kaufmann, Marc Kipfer, Mike Kirk, Jen Kushell, Don Lee, Phil Lempert, Gert van Manan, Pat Mitchell, Juan Carlos Rojas, Jack Schwartz, Errol Schweizer, Ben Silverman, Dr. Charles Sims, Diane Snyder, Tim Sperry, Art Volkman, Michael Miqueli, and Alfredo Liranzo.

Thank you to the friends I made in Pittsburgh, Marquette, Peace Corps, Duke, and the ones Maura and I made in North Carolina, Memphis, El Salvador, New York, Redondo Beach, and so many places around the world. I have been influenced by all of you for the better. A special mention to my partners at Powerplant Ventures, Kevin Boylan, T. K. Pillan, and Dan Beldy for dealing with my crazy writing schedule over the last two years.

Thank you to the thousands of people across the tropical world who have dedicated their time, effort, and resources to plant, cultivate, harvest, and process the wonderful coconuts that make Zico what it is. There would be no Zico without you and no fruit for which to reach higher.

There are two final groups to thank. To the retailers of all different shapes, sizes, and countries, thank you for believing in Zico and giving us a way to reach our consumers. Finally, to the millions of Zico drinkers, thank you for making space in your crowded lives for our little brand. You made this all possible and for that I will be forever grateful. I hope you will keep Zico as part of your lives but more importantly reach higher yourselves in everything you do.

INDEX